UNSTUCK

Break Free.
Rise Up.
Launch Out.

RICHARD PERINCHIEF

AVAIL

WHAT PEOPLE ARE SAYING ABOUT *UNSTUCK*

Unstuck is a masterpiece of wisdom and faith. Move yourself and others through any situation you are facing in life in great victory! I highly recommend this magnificent liberating new book by pastor and author Richard Perinchief!

—Bob Weiner
Weiner Ministries International
Gainesville, Florida

I have known pastor and author Richard Perinchief for over thirty years and have found him to be a phenomenal communicator. He has shown openness and willingness to change and has a great perspective on being able to recognize when you are stuck—yet have the determination and skills to get through it. I encourage every person, no matter your stage of life, to read *Unstuck* and put its contents into practice as they will give you the ability to break out of your current reality and step into your next!

—Steve Kelly
Senior Pastor of Wave Church
Virginia Beach, Virginia

I have a high appreciation for instructional teaching that brings forth practical theology in the atmosphere of God's supernatural provision. That is why *Unstuck* contains real value for anyone who reads it.

Pastor and author Richard Perinchief opens his heart and shares over thirty years of ministry and daily life experiences. These are real situations where the circumstances can appear (at times) overwhelming, and life can seem to have us "boxed in."

It is through these experiences that God has given Pastor Perinchief biblical insight and understanding on how we can confront our own times of being "stuck," and break free from their causes and negative effects in such a way that we become empowered to help others.

—Dr. Jerry Williamson
President, Go To Nations
Jacksonville, Florida

It takes time, testing, transparency, and truth to be qualified to promote the change necessary to break free from the state of being STUCK. All people experience being stuck, but not all escape its grip.

Pastor and author Richard Perinchief has artfully and honestly tackled the topic without pretense or compromise. His approach is at once compassionate and straightforward. If you are ready and you read it, *Unstuck* will not only initiate the process but help you navigate forward into your freedom-filled future.

—*Michael Pitts*
Bishop and Founder, Cornerstone Global Network
Toledo, Ohio

Unstuck is absolutely eye-opening—an awesome read! Pastor and author Richard Perinchief gives practical insight to help believers move forward in their God-given purpose. In a conversational style, he clearly brings the reader to a point of introspection so that hindrances are removed, and positive momentum is ignited. Pastor Richard transparently shares his own life stories to help illuminate the snares that entrap many people, along with the solutions to prevent and escape them. You will be taken on a journey that brings tears to your eyes, joy to your soul, and motivation to your heart. *Unstuck* is a treasure trove of knowledge, principles, and learned wisdom that will equip any individual to overcome the common adversities and challenges that all experience. It will help all who read it to get unstuck, and I highly recommend this life-changing book!

—*Pastor Dr. Robert Gay*
Senior Pastor and Founder, High Praise Worship Center
Panama City, Florida

What an absolutely relatable subject regarding where we are in the world today—STUCK! How many of us, myself included, have been there and felt just that way? Pastor and author Richard Perinchief's insightful stories and relatable facts make *Unstuck* a must-read for everyone. This book has challenged me to live an unstuck life. Thanks, Richard!

—*Bert Wimberly*
Senior Pastor and Founder, Gates of the City Church
Kerrville, Texas

There is so much fear in our lives. *Unstuck* walks us through so many situations that you and I are afraid to confront. Pastor and author Richard Perinchief's personal stories encourage us to put our trust in God and discover freedom in Him. It is not often we can read such an honest and personal account. After reading *Unstuck*, you will not feel condemned, but you will be encouraged to look for more. Don't be afraid of it.

—*Zibi Marzec*
Pastor, The Church for the City of Krakow
Krakow, Poland

Nothing gives credibility as much as **fruitful** longevity does! After three decades of LIVING life with pastor and author Richard Perinchief, I've had the honor of becoming a true spiritual son. With that privilege, I've also gotten to see firsthand some of the sacrifice it's taken to own these truths! That's why I'm so thrilled to add my YES to *Unstuck*! It's not just a bunch of theories—it's life-changing, proven wisdom from a man who has proven character! I know so many lives are going to be impacted! What a perfect tool to help people get *UN*stuck!

—Lindsey Seals
Senior Associate and Worship Pastor, NOW Church
Ocala, Florida

Unstuck couldn't be more timely. Written largely from his life's experiences, pastor and author Richard Perinchief takes a straight and honest look at the things which so easily cause many of us to get stuck where we don't really want to be. Rather than simply being a book to inspire and ignite personal vision, *Unstuck* will cause you to draw nearer to God whilst fanning into flame the things He has deposited in your life. If you're sensing that the Holy Spirit is stirring something new inside, that there is more to your life or ministry than where you have currently ended up, then I encourage you to read *Unstuck* and step boldly into the new season God has prepared.

—Julian Melfi
Senior Pastor, Citygate Church
London, UK

I am privileged to have pastor and author Richard Perinchief as *my* pastor for over three decades—thirty-plus years of adventures in faith! He has led us with wisdom and spiritual strength, navigating our church and family through challenging times and into abundant fulfillment. In *Unstuck*, he shares God-revealed, time-tested truth that has the power to get you through stuck seasons into a God-designed life!

—Chris Hays
Associate Pastor, NOW Church
Ocala, Florida

What an adventure—*Unstuck*! Each of us has experienced being stuck in different areas of life. *Unstuck* reflects the heart of pastor and author Richard Perinchief, who—in my opinion, and the opinions of thousands of people—is a blessing for the church of the world. Masterfully and in a simple way, Pastor Richard lets us see principles based on the Word of God, resulting from his vast experience as a communicator of the Word and pastor for more than thirty years. *Unstuck* is not only devotional reading, but it can also be a manual for leaders or a small-group guide.

—Manny Cabezudo
Pastor, City Church
Ocala, Florida

With a refreshing combination of sincerity, wisdom, and personal experience, pastor and author Richard Perinchief shares inspiring stories of how he and his wife, Gail, bravely stepped into the life God was calling them into. If you're ready to live in freedom, get unstuck, and step into the fulfillment your heart has been aching for, *Unstuck* is right on time.

—Kevin Green
Senior Pastor, Airborne Church
Martinsburg, West Virginia

A book is only as good as the person writing it. I have known pastor and author Richard Perinchief for over two decades, so I knew this would be a good book. *Unstuck* is not just the title of this work, but it is also what you will become after reading the powerful principles and faith-building stories shared throughout its pages. I'm so glad that Richard has taken the time to document these truths that will help us all live lives of freedom.

—Dr. Dave Martin
Author, Success Coach, and Pastor
Troy, Michigan

I cannot recommend *Unstuck* highly enough. Pastor and author Richard Perinchief is an apostolic master builder who writes from his heart, scriptural revelation, and his personal journey of going from stuck to unstuck. Perinchief's discovered wisdom will get you moving on the path of your God-given assignment and destiny!

—John P. Kelly
Convening Apostle, International Coalition of Apostolic Leaders
Fort Worth, Texas

The principles and real-life stories in *Unstuck* are sure to guide you through even the sludgiest of seasons. That is exactly what has happened in our marriage and parenting and as pastors of a local church. Pastor and author Richard Perinchief's gift is one of invitation and teaching. Through anecdotes from his life, he invites you into a world that is so much greater with Jesus. Get ready to move forward and live UNSTUCK!

—Matt Erikson
Pastor and Founder, Mercy City Church
Lincoln, Nebraska

Reading *Unstuck* is like sitting down with a wise father, learning from his experience. I have personally benefited from pastor and author Richard Perinchief's wisdom and guidance for the last twenty-five years. *Unstuck* is full of many of the stories and lessons I have learned to keep me from getting stuck and continuing to move forward in all God has for me.

—Carrie Erikson
Co-Pastor and Founder, Mercy City Church
Lincoln, Nebraska

In *Unstuck*, pastor and author Richard Perinchief pulls back the curtain to not only give the practical tools but also lend his personal stories to help you and me truly LIVE a forward-focused God-purposed life!

—Damon Moore
Senior Pastor, City Place Church
Orlando, Florida

The body of Christ is struggling to find its identity. We all get stuck in one area of life or another; our ancestors in the faith did, too. God wants His people to find freedom. The question is, are we willing to learn *how* to get unstuck? Pastor and author Richard Perinchief's *Unstuck* provides a dynamic glimpse of the power God's church can wield when we help one another walk in our God-given freedom!

—Martijn van Tilborgh
Strategic Marketing Architect and Consultant
Sanford, Florida

Honest, authentic, and relevant . . . in *Unstuck*, pastor and author Richard Perinchief takes us on a journey of personal self-discovery while providing real-world specific steps to get unstuck in any of life's predicaments. Richard does a fantastic job of weaving in poignant parts of scripture to validate points, almost as a Bible companion to solve complicated decisions. I was most struck by Richard's vulnerability in sharing detailed personal stories of being stuck himself, only to reveal that he had to embrace his faith to make positive life changes—the one true way to get unstuck in this life.

—Jim Knight
Keynote Speaker, Podcaster and Best-Selling Author, *Culture That Rocks*

Ever felt stuck struggling to see progress in your life? You're not alone! Pastor Richard reminds us that being stuck happens to us all but staying stuck is a choice. This book will breathe hope back into your world and revive the dreams you once had. Learning to trust God through His process, you too can begin moving forward with renewed purpose!

—Chad C. Braswell
Senior Pastor of Metro Church
Marlborough, Massachusetts

Copyright © 2022 by Richard Perinchief

Published by AVAIL

All rights reserved. No portion of this book may be reproduced, stored in a retrieval system, or transmitted in any form or by any means—electronic, mechanical, photocopy, recording, scanning, or other—except for brief quotations in critical reviews or articles, without prior written permission of the author.

Scripture quotations marked NIV are taken from the Holy Bible, New International Version®, NIV®. Copyright © 1973, 1978, 1984, 2011 by Biblica, Inc.™ Used by permission of Zondervan. All rights reserved worldwide. www.zondervan.com. The "NIV" and "New International Version" are trademarks registered in the United States Patent and Trademark Office by Biblica, Inc.™ | Scripture quotations marked NKJV are taken from the New King James Version®. Copyright © 1982 by Thomas Nelson. Used by permission. All rights reserved. | Scripture quotations marked NLT are taken from the Holy Bible, New Living Translation, copyright © 1996, 2004, 2015 by Tyndale House Foundation. Used by permission of Tyndale House Publishers, Inc., Carol Stream, Illinois 60188. All rights reserved. | Scripture quotations marked MSG are taken from THE MESSAGE, copyright © 1993, 1994, 1995, 1996, 2000, 2001, 2002 by Eugene H. Peterson. Used by permission of NavPress. All rights reserved. Represented by Tyndale House Publishers, Inc. | Scripture quotations marked TPT are from The Passion Translation®. Copyright © 2017, 2018 by Passion & Fire Ministries, Inc. Used by permission. All rights reserved. ThePassionTranslation.com. | All Scripture marked with the designation GW is taken from GOD'S WORD®. © 1995, 2003, 2013, 2014, 2019, 2020 by God's Word to the Nations Mission Society. Used by permission. | Copyright © 2015 by The Lockman Foundation, La Habra, CA 90631. All rights reserved. The "Amplified" trademark (AMP) is registered in the United States Patent and Trademark Office by The Lockman Foundation. Use of this trademark requires the permission of The Lockman Foundation.

For foreign and subsidiary rights, contact the author.

Cover design by: Sara Young

Cover Photo by: Andrew van Tilborgh

ISBN: 978-1-957369-84-6   1 2 3 4 5 6 7 8 9 10

Printed in the United States of America

DEDICATION

My five grandchildren each continually add so much joy to my life, and I would like to dedicate this book to them. Cole inspires me with his creativity and wisdom. Caden encourages me with his big hugs and his huge passion for life. Mila impacts me with her positivity and imagination. Alana's sweetness and gentle spirit always make me smile. And Kylynn dazzles me with her laughter and playfulness. I pray that each of these precious seeds will live their lives for Jesus, to the fullness of God's purpose, using their great talents and humor to always move forward, from stuck to unstuck.

SPECIAL THANKS

I want to thank everyone who made this book possible, starting with my amazing wife, Gail, and my awesome family. There is something so special about being called to do life and ministry together. I want to express my love and gratitude to Ricky and Jenny Perinchief, as well as Kristen and Tristan Kennedy, our precious and hardworking children. Without their support, I could never have done this.

Thank you, also, to my incredible NOW Church family—particularly the pastors and staff. God teaches me so much through all of you, and it is my honor to be your pastor as we follow The Lord together.

And all my gratitude to my excellent publishing team, especially my longtime friend John Mason. John has been an amazing friend, trusted confidant, and blessing to my life and ministry for many years, and when he brought in my editor, Joshua Lease, I knew that we had a great team put together. Also, Nancy Blackman has played such an important role in keeping this project moving forward.

I'd also like to mention other key individuals, including Martijn Van Tilborgh and Debbie Chand, as well as the Erikson family and their wonderful people at Mercy City Church in Lincoln, Nebraska—who all believed in this project, encouraged me, and helped to make it happen.

CONTENTS

Foreword xv

Introduction 17

CHAPTER 1. Stuck Happens 19

CHAPTER 2. Ditch Your Dead Moseses 35

CHAPTER 3. The Lies Hold Us Back 51

CHAPTER 4. Your Burning Bush Moment 65

CHAPTER 5. Show Your Scars 77

CHAPTER 6. Generations of Freedom 87

CHAPTER 7. Out of Your Control 101

CHAPTER 8. Where Are You? 113

CHAPTER 9. Supernatural, Not Superhuman 125

CHAPTER 10. Tune In 139

CHAPTER 11. Discerning His Voice 147

CHAPTER 12. That or Better 163

CHAPTER 13. Show Them How to Be Free 179

FOREWORD

If there ever were people who exemplified living the unstuck life, they would be Richard Perinchief and his wife, Gail. Having known both for more than thirty years as pastors in a local church and ministers around the world, I've had a front-row seat to their incredible journey of helping thousands of people discover lasting freedom.

This book is about more than getting unstuck; it's an introduction to the only One who can help you stay free—God. This book instructs you through good times and bad, draws from Bible legends who were stuck, shows how God still used them, and describes Richard and Gail's miraculous God-adventures worldwide.

Richard is one of the most determined, God-honoring persons I know. His insights will help you to not only grow in your persistence but also to never stop going after God's best. Whatever has held you captive, liberty is coming your way.

Freedom is one of the most neglected promises from God for believers, but that is about to change. You are about to discover how to be unstuck—free to be and do what God has planned for you. The old saying is true, "You can't be anything you want to be, but you can be everything God wants you to be."

—John Mason
Author of *An Enemy Called Average*
and numerous other bestselling books

INTRODUCTION

When God set me on the path to writing a book, I had no idea that He would direct me toward a topic that's not only pertinent and timely but also a message that has found its way into my life and teaching for decades. If you look back at my messages over the course of more than thirty years, you'll see the genesis of this book's formation and a life

Getting unstuck.

We all get stuck. I know it's certainly happened to me many times throughout my life. As I write this, we're coming through one of the biggest crises in decades. Still, while it would be easy to focus on the impact that a global pandemic has had on people, stunting their forward motion, the truth is that "stuck" can happen anytime, in good circumstances or bad ones.

Stuck isn't limited to pandemics, global financial crises, or personal life events that can feel crippling. Stuck can happen when business seems good, when your relationship is humming along, or even when you feel close to God. It can happen to non-Christians and Christians alike.

Our reasons for feeling stuck are as varied as we are, and we'll talk about some of them in this book. But, first, I'm going to share some of my personal stories of being stuck—and, more importantly, getting *un*stuck.

I believe it's possible to recognize the things that block your way, confront those situations in faith, and break out of your inner confinement. But the fact is, getting unstuck isn't just about you. So I'm not only going to give you a path for getting freedom for yourself but also a method for how to share it with others.

As we get started, I want you to understand this: if you feel stuck, it doesn't mean something is wrong with you. Some of the greatest

stories of the Bible revolve around people who were stuck and—more importantly—the God who set them and sets us free.

God knows we get stuck. He's done incredible things through people prone to being stuck, just like you and me. Fortunately for us, He doesn't leave us there.

> **IT IS MY PRAYER THAT THROUGH THIS BOOK, GOD WILL SHOW YOU NOT ONLY HOW TO GET UNSTUCK BUT ALSO HOW TO LIVE A LIFE OF FREEDOM AND GET UNSTUCK THE NEXT TIME YOU FIND YOURSELF THERE.**

It is my prayer that through this book, God will show you not only how to get unstuck but also how to live a life of freedom and get unstuck the next time you find yourself there. Yes, that's right, it will happen again. Yet instead of dreading the next time, you're going to have a framework for how God sets us free in the context of a relationship with Him through His Holy Spirit.

The question you must ask yourself is if you are willing to learn how God gets us unstuck so that you can help both yourself and others.

If you're willing, then let's dive in! It's time to get unstuck.

CHAPTER 1

STUCK HAPPENS

I've been stuck plenty of times. Some of my earliest childhood memories are of lying in bed in the middle of the night, wheezing from asthma and unable to catch my breath. With my head propped up on pillows, my mother rubbed Vicks VapoRub on my chest. I spent too many sleepless nights, and sometimes days, trapped in my room, mostly alone and wondering if my coughing would ever stop. *Will I ever just be able to take a normal deep breath without choking and sputtering?* I wondered. Thankfully, God even intervened in that and healed me in adulthood.

Once, as a teenager, I drove my first car (a yellow 1975 Dodge Dart Sport) to my favorite beach with a couple of friends. New Smyrna Beach, Florida, was only forty-five minutes from where I grew up, and you could *drive* and park right along the ocean on the sand. Unfortunately, I underestimated how soft the sand was and wound up getting STUCK, *spinning my wheels* trying frantically to get myself out but just getting *deeper*. I was so embarrassed in front of my buddies; thankfully, some guys with a big pickup truck came by and offered to help. But I learned an important life lesson that day. Sometimes you need *somebody else* with the right equipment to help you get unstuck.

Being stuck is one of the worst feelings in the world. If you've ever seen a documentary on cave exploring, you may have seen brave men

# UNSTUCK

and women worm their way into a crack or crevice that doesn't seem much bigger than their heads. Then, pushing a light ahead of them, they creep and crawl forward, hoping that the crack will open up into a new passage. But what happens when they can't go any further ahead? And—this is why I could never be a cave explorer—what if they find they can't go back, either?

I've never gotten stuck while exploring a cave, but I have gotten stuck in life, where you can't seem to find a way forward, and you don't feel like you can go back. Sometimes you don't even know the way ahead because it's all dark and hidden from your sight.

As Christians, "stuck" can seem especially bad. Aren't we expected to have the *answers*? Isn't God supposed to show us the path, so we can walk it? If you're like me, it's particularly frustrating to think that all the answers you need are seemingly just a prayer away . . . so why does it sometimes feel like your prayers for direction or help fall on deaf ears?

Many things make us feel stuck, and we'll talk about some of them. I feel like I have unique insight on this because, honestly, I've been stuck a lot. That may surprise you that a pastor has felt stuck a lot. Aren't we the ones with the hotline to the throne room of God? We're supposed to have "Spidey senses" and spirits connected to the very mind of God, right?

> **I FEEL LIKE I HAVE UNIQUE INSIGHT ON BEING STUCK BECAUSE, HONESTLY, I'VE BEEN STUCK A LOT.**

Well, I'll let you in on a bit of a secret—pastors feel stuck too. A lot! And here's another confession: I'm not going to offer you a silver bullet. Nope, there is no formula that, in four easy steps, will get you unstuck every time.

Instead, my desire here is to introduce you to Someone who can always get you unstuck. You see, God is never stuck. He is the definition of freedom. The solution to being stuck isn't working a formula; it's knowing a Person. If you're already a Christian, right now, you might be tempted to dismiss this because I already mentioned that Christians can be stuck just like anyone else. What's the difference? I'm so glad you asked! The truth is, it's not enough to just have the title of Christian. God desires something for you, a level of relationship and connection, that doesn't come just by warming the chair in a church. By the time you're done with this book, you're going to see *how* God sets you free, and you'll understand how to meaningfully connect with His Spirit to seek answers and freedom no matter how stuck you've become.

"You're too excited about the Lord." Those words came to me during one of the worst seasons of being stuck in my life.

I felt trapped between the person God was calling me to be and the person the world was trying to press me into. At twenty-two, I was in the insurance business, but I felt this call to something else—ministry. I was saved in the evangelical Presbyterian church, and I never thought that God would call me to preach in a million years. I got an early start in life, marrying young and having two small kids by the time I was twenty-two, but I felt this passion for God I simply couldn't explain.

So much so, a guy took me to lunch one day to tell me, "Look, you need to calm down. You're too excited about the Lord." That's right, you can be too excited about God—at least according to that guy. He had been to seminary, had thought he would be a pastor, and now found himself in the insurance industry. "You're already in insurance," he told me. "You're probably just supposed to be a big giver."

Because that's where life had taken him, he thought that is what I should do, too. He wanted me in the same box he was in. But when I

thought about this, a trapped feeling descended on me. I was conflicted because I felt this call of God but was really good at insurance sales. I had never dreamed of being a pastor, I hadn't completed college, and I had a family to provide for. Also, let's just say the path to being a Presbyterian minister wasn't exactly exciting. Yet, I felt that's exactly what God was calling me to (but I didn't yet understand that sometimes God calls us to something before revealing He has an even better plan in mind than we think).

I took this man's words to heart and tried to be content with what he had said over me. Yet, as I did so and took my eye off what God was calling me to, the faucet of provision that had flown so freely through my insurance business faltered. It was like God cut off the flow just a little.

I felt like I was to preach, but the words I'd heard, what I thought I had to do, and what God was calling me to didn't match up.

I didn't know who I was. One thing I *did* know—I was *stuck*.

I believe this represents the entire body of Christ on one level or another. I meet so many Christians who struggle with their identity and who do not know what it looks like to be the people God made them to be. But before you think that I believe we're all supposed to be pastors or missionaries, that is not what I mean at all.

We are all new creations in Christ—but many of us struggle to understand and live out precisely what that means. Paul wrote, "Now, if anyone is enfolded into Christ, he has become an entirely new person. All that is related to the old order has vanished. Behold, everything is fresh and new" (2 Corinthians 5:17, TPT). You are not just what you were. No matter your personality or experiences, you have a spiritual component that is quickened and made alive when you come to know Jesus Christ as your personal Lord and Savior. He enables you to think differently, see differently, and live differently.

He sets you free.

If you don't know who you are, I guarantee you're going to feel stuck. If you don't understand what God has done for you in Jesus and that you're made new from the inside out, you risk staying mired in the old ways of thinking, seeing, and living that leave people feeling trapped and unable to move forward in their lives, calling, and relationship with God.

Many of us wrestle with the big question about who we are. It's not just an issue for teens trying to discover their identity. As a pastor, I meet people in their twenties who are wondering if they'll have lives as good as the ones their parents had. I talk with people in the middle of their lives, and they wonder how they got where they are. I even meet older people who wonder what happened to their lives and if there's anything left for them at their age. They thought their lives would be different, and they're disappointed that their youthful dreams of what life would be like and even what God would do have fallen flat or ground to a standstill. All different types and ages of people feel stuck and unsure about moving forward or what God has for their lives.

You may be wondering where that leaves you when you're on the wrong side of all the mistakes you've made and the disappointments you've experienced or even outright disobedience you've lived in. You may feel that you'll never get on the right path or that it's too late. You're disqualified, under-equipped, too tired, too scared, or just too uncertain to find the fulfillment you seek in life.

Does that sound like you? Are you one of the many—one of *us*—who question what God's plan is and if you're ever going to be able to get unstuck and move forward past *surviving* and into *thriving*? Past being directionless and trapped so you can move into the rewarding purpose for which you've been created? If so, you picked up the right book—not because of me and how great I am but because I've been there. And God led me out, over and over again.

You see, "When God chooses someone and graciously imparts gifts to him, they are never rescinded" (Romans 11:29, TPT). That's right. He has given you unique and wonderful gifts that equip you to do something great on this earth—and He will never change His

mind on blessing you. You're not an accident or a mistake—you're a divinely crafted masterpiece made by our heavenly Father for relationship with Him and for the good works He knows you're capable of doing.

> **HELPING PEOPLE FIND THEIR DESTINY AND PURPOSE HAS BEEN A CORE ELEMENT OF MY MINISTRY FOR OVER THREE DECADES, AND I AM ENTIRELY CONVINCED THAT YOU ARE WHERE YOU ARE RIGHT NOW FOR A REASON.**

Helping people find their destiny and purpose has been a core element of my ministry for over three decades, and I am entirely convinced that you are where you are *right now* for a reason. You may feel trapped, uncertain, exhausted, or just unsure who you are or why you're here. But God knew you before you were in your mother's womb, and He had the most fulfilling, amazing plan for your life worked out before you even drew your first breath!

Wouldn't you like to know how to walk in it?

In these pages, you're going to discover how God sees you, what He has done for you in Jesus, and what that means. You are His workmanship—His masterpiece—created in Jesus to do the good things He has prepared for you. Ephesians 2:10 (TPT) describes it like this:

> *We have become his poetry, a re-created people that will fulfill the destiny he has given each of us, for we are joined to Jesus, the Anointed One. Even before we were born, God planned in advance our destiny and the good works we would do to fulfill it!*

Yet through it all, He has chosen to preserve our free will. So how can it be both that He has a plan and that we have the ability to make

RICHARD PERINCHIEF

decisions like our Father? It's because His purpose is in line with the desires of your heart. As your loving Father, He knew what would move you, what would stir your passion, and He has a plan for you that will both draw that out of you and fulfill His will for you on earth.

At twenty-two, I didn't know that yet.

I knew in the church where I was saved and discipled that there were only two things to do if you felt "called by God." First, I could go the seminary route to Jackson, Mississippi, for a couple of years, then intern for a year or so, and wind up hoping and praying for a chance to get started as a children's pastor by the time I was thirty. Or I could be a missionary to some faraway country, likely without running water.

Honestly, laid out like that, it didn't seem very appealing.

Learning that these options were what my church could offer felt like a gut punch. Maybe I *was* just supposed to be in insurance and a big giver after all. I was confused, and I was definitely stuck.

With those as apparently the only options for ministry, I pivoted toward focusing on my insurance business, deciding I'd just be involved in my local church. I quickly became the head usher, and later I became the youngest deacon in the history of that church. That'd be enough for God, right?

Part of the problem was that the leaders of my church could *see* the call of God on my life, but they only had this narrow interpretation of what that could look like. And what I felt in my heart didn't line up with their formula. Meanwhile, insurance was rocking and rolling. I was promoted to sales manager, had five people older than me working under me, and my company was fast-tracking me. They wanted me to go to the home office, become a teacher and trainer of agents, and climb the corporate ladder. In 1986, I finished first in my district, number two in the state of Florida, and number twenty-nine in the whole country!

So, from 1983 to 1987, I just focused on being a big giver in my local church. I was leaning into God and going after my relationship with

Him. But despite remarkable success in insurance, I also had these periods I mentioned where it was like the faucet got turned off. Then, as soon as that would happen, I would think, *It's because I'm **supposed to be a pastor**.*

There just didn't seem to be a way forward. I even tried to go to seminary like others wanted me to, but it was a nonstarter. That wasn't in my heart, and the door didn't open at all. I was knocking on it, but nothing was opening up.

That is, until God blew my mind, opened up my eyes, and stretched my thinking, as only He can. I had believed the call of God on my life was limited to the picture that had been painted for me—an insurance big-giver or a long-haul slog through seminary on my way to being a pastor in my denomination. But what if neither of those was the path God had for me? What if He had something else—something, dare I say, *better*?

Right now, you may only see one path forward—or three bad ones, or none at all. As you imagine that future, it doesn't bring you peace or feel *right*. Perhaps someone has painted that picture for you, trying to force you to live in their preconceptions for your life. This could be from an individual or even a group, like my church's denomination. Yet their plan for your life just doesn't seem like it fits. Maybe you've even put a "God" label on it as I did in assuming that the call of God could only look like the ministry plan my church offered me.

No one's plan for your life is as good as God's. And He is not up in heaven cooking up something for your life that you're not going to like. However, He does have a plan for each of us. He describes it like this: "I know what I'm doing. I have it all planned out—plans to take care of you, not abandon you, plans to give you the future you hope for" (Jeremiah 29:11, MSG). He knows what He's doing, and we can trust Him implicitly. God will never leave us or abandon us, and the plan He has for our lives is designed to give us hope.

RICHARD PERINCHIEF

> **NO ONE'S PLAN FOR YOUR LIFE IS AS GOOD AS GOD'S. AND HE IS NOT UP IN HEAVEN COOKING UP SOMETHING FOR YOUR LIFE THAT YOU'RE NOT GOING TO LIKE.**

How does that feel? *Hope.* Just savor that idea for a moment. *HOPE!*

I didn't know it in December of 1986, but God was about to show my wife, Gail, and me our path forward, our hope, and it wasn't anything we could've predicted.

I grew up and was saved in a denomination that was very closed to the things of the Holy Spirit. So, the only charismatic person my wife and I knew was my "crazy aunt from New Jersey"—and, yes, that's exactly what we called her! But the thing was, we also knew that she had a hotline to heaven because when she prayed . . . she got *answers!*

We lived in Ocala, Florida, but we heard from Auntie Marilyn about a large charismatic church about seventy miles away. So, we decided to visit close to Christmas time. Leaving our kids with a babysitter, we drove over there with my in-laws. And we loved it! Yet seventy miles was a long way to drive for church, especially with two little kids. So could God really be calling us to go there?

We started making the drive, and at one meeting, the pastor announced a healing service. We didn't know what that meant, but we decided to go. At one point during that special service, the pastor said, "Maybe you don't need a physical healing; maybe your miracle is something else. Tell God what you need right now."

That really hit me. I prayed, *Lord, before I leave this room, I just want to know if I'm called to be a pastor or a businessman. That's all I want to know; if I can get that answer, that's my miracle.*

STUCK

Being from conservative denominations, my wife and I had never seen what we witnessed at that church during that service! People were getting healed, and some were even *falling over*! This was unlike anything we'd ever seen, but it was obvious God was doing *something*.

Near the end of the service, the pastor said, "If you felt the power of God, get down here to the altar right now!" So I hopped up and actually ran to the front and got in a line of people. The pastor was going down the line, touching people, and many were falling over. I watched some of them obviously setting themselves up to fall over easily, rocking back on their heels. Now, I wanted more of God, but I was still very *Presbyterian*, and I still had all that in me. I *braced myself*—no way this guy was pushing *me* over!

As he came by, he didn't push. He just barely brushed my head . . . and down I went like a bag of cement, flat on my rear!

The pastor finished the line of people at the front, and then he did something very unusual. He came back to *me*. Standing over me, he said, "God is going to use this young man. This guy is going to be a pastor, and he's going to preach all over the world."

I burst into tears! My wife and mother-in-law were behind me, and they heard what he said as well. I could hear them sobbing, too because they knew how trapped I had felt for the last few years.

With that one move of the Holy Spirit, God answered the burning desire in my heart. I had my epiphany. I'd received my answer to the questions I'd asked for years:

"Who am I?"

"What am I supposed to do?"

"What did You make me to be?"

Are you asking questions like these? Do you want to know your identity in Christ, your purpose and destiny? Do you want to get off high-center and start living the life God has designed you for?

Maybe you've asked these questions before, and you find yourself doing so now—stuck *again*. Unanswered, these questions can be like splinters in our hearts, making us uncomfortable in our own skins. Maybe the options before you all seem like bad choices, or you feel like you have *no options at all*. Perhaps you think God is asking something of you that you do not want.

If that's you, I actually suggest you take a break from those questions. The solution you seek isn't a formula or a method that will get you unstuck; it's connecting with the One who has the answers. It's time to pray and ask God for an encounter with Him and His Holy Spirit that will give you not just the breakthrough you need right now but the connection with Him that will allow you to get breakthrough after breakthrough.

It's not the answers that you need. It's the *One* who *has* the solutions—He is who you need. And we're going to explore how to connect with Him together!

I come from a long line of Perinchiefs who served the Lord.

My dad was a music minister, but my grandfather was a Methodist pastor, and my great grandfather was a Methodist pastor. At least ten of the last fifteen generations in my family have been ministers, dating back to the 1600s.

I felt that weight as a kid, but all I wanted to be was a rock 'n' roll star. I definitely didn't want to be a pastor! My earliest memory of even thinking about what pastors do was around fourteen when, with my hair grown down to my shoulders, I was sitting with my grandfather perhaps a year before he died. I can remember asking him, "Why would you be a pastor? That's got to be the dullest thing imaginable." He didn't take it poorly, even though my teenage self had delivered it so tactlessly, and began telling me about the call of God.

I remember it actually scared me a little bit because I wasn't even saved then. Yet as I look back on it, I now realize that this feeling I had in my chest that scared me as a teenager was a calling and purpose of God that wouldn't receive its answer until that healing service so many years later. I can now see that some of the things I did growing

up were trying to run from that feeling that was welling up inside me when I talked to my grandfather. For example, I went a little sideways in high school because I had this notion that if I did enough bad stuff, I wouldn't have to be a pastor. After all, pastors are holy people, so if I smoked pot or drank with my friends, then I would be disqualified, and God would leave me alone.

Right? Wrong! The gifts and callings of God don't get rescinded, and you are never disqualified from the purpose God has for you!

I didn't want to be a pastor as a teen. However, my aptitude test and guidance counselor (who went to our church) painted a clear picture of what I would be good at. He said it would be one of three things: a lawyer, a broadcast journalist, or a pastor. He told me he had never seen such an obvious result on an aptitude test!

I told him that we could scratch off the pastor thing from the list; I would *never* do that. Then I asked him how much schooling it took to be a lawyer, and he told me. Scratch that one, too! So, I thought I would be a broadcast journalist, but I somehow ended up selling insurance—and feeling incredibly divided. I didn't know *what* I was supposed to be or *who* I was supposed to be.

I felt like I was late to the party and trying to figure it out. I felt like everyone else around me already knew, but I still hadn't figured out what I wanted to be when I grew up.

As I got older, I felt divided between two things (insurance and the call God had put on my life), and I wasn't having fulfilling success at either of them. I had not yet discovered how to connect with God and receive His wisdom or that I needed to trust Him without wavering instead of being a person of divided loyalty. When we are what the Bible calls "double-minded," our commitment is divided between God and the world, and we are unstable in everything we do. When we are like that, we can't expect to receive the wisdom of God.

Maybe you're a little bit like me, conflicted and divided and unsure what direction to go. Perhaps you have a preconception of what serving God will look like. But, whether your attitudes are shaped by your church, your biases, or even your fears, believe me when I say that it may not look anything like you dread it will. In fact, I would argue the opposite—serving God is the most fulfilling thing that a person can do.

Later, we will talk about how being called to serve God doesn't always look like what we may think of as "ministry." I'll give you my definition of what ministry is then, but for right now, it's enough to understand that *every believer* is called to serve God and to minister in some way. However, relatively few of us end up in "the ministry." And that's a good thing. God doesn't need you to do what I do; He wants you to do what He has uniquely equipped and prepared *you* to do.

> **GOD DOESN'T NEED YOU TO DO WHAT OTHER PEOPLE DO; HE WANTS YOU TO DO WHAT HE HAS UNIQUELY EQUIPPED AND PREPARED YOU TO DO.**

I believe within each of us is a passion that will bring us unequaled fulfillment and glorify God. For me, it was becoming a pastor. However, God has equipped you to do something better than anyone else—something He has called you to do that is as unique as you are. He's made something easy to you that doesn't come naturally to others or something that only you are strategically positioned to do. I believe that within you is a call—a call you cannot escape because God's goodness and tender love will pursue you all the days of your life.

In Psalm 37:4 (NKJV), David wrote, "Delight yourself also in the Lord, and He shall give you the desires of your heart." Now, on the face of it, you can read this and say that God will give you the things

you desire. However, what if *God* is the one who put those desires in your heart? What if He placed in your heart the very things you want most because He knows they will bring you the greatest fulfillment *and* glorify Him?

That would mean that it's safe to trust Him with your life. That would mean that He has a plan for you that will give you hope and a bright future. He knows what He's doing; He has it planned out, and He will always see His plan and His word come to fruition. He began this good thing in you, and He will give you a hope-filled future.

If you feel stuck, before we go any further, it's time to pull out all of those things that you'd hoped for—yes, even the dreams that seem dead—and lay them down before God. If God put it in you, it's not over yet. Even if your life feels like it's in broken pieces, spread them out before the living God and watch Him put them back together as only He can.

If you're still alive, it's not over. No matter how stuck you feel, God will never leave you or forsake you, and He is faithful to complete that which He starts.

Freedom and release are coming, but here's the thing—they come in the context of a relationship with God. As we will see, the singular advice I can give you to get unstuck now, live in freedom, and get unstuck again in the future is found in your *relationship* with our loving heavenly Father.

He hasn't offered us a formula, and I'm not offering you one, either. Instead, God—right now, right where you are, no matter your current circumstances—has wide-open arms for you. He wants you to get to know Him as He knows you, to speak with you and help you. He wants to set you free in every area of your life because we serve a God of freedom. Jesus came to set each one of us free from being stuck, and whom the Son sets free is free indeed.

RICHARD PERINCHIEF

> **JESUS CAME TO SET EACH ONE OF US FREE FROM BEING STUCK, AND WHOM THE SON SETS FREE IS FREE INDEED.**

So, if you're ready to leave the ideas of magic bullets behind and, instead, pursue a connection with God that will help you live the life you dream of, it's time to take your next step.

It's time to leave behind all your dead Moseses, so you can step into what's next—the Promised Land.

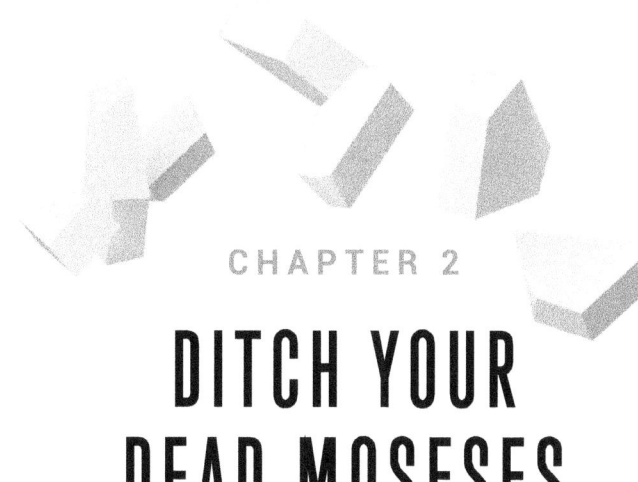

CHAPTER 2

DITCH YOUR DEAD MOSESES

At the beginning of the book of Joshua in the Bible, God made a seemingly rhetorical statement to Joshua. Moses had died—God knew he was dead; Joshua knew Moses was dead. All of Israel knew. So why did God bother to say, "Moses My servant is dead. Now therefore, arise, go"? (Joshua 1:2, NKJV)

Now, if you just read the Bible like some other book, you might think that this was just filler the author wrote to sound official and, well, biblical. However, if you read the Bible like it's God's perfect Word, you've got to look at every single word and ask yourself why it's there. What's the point?

I believe God was trying to convey to Joshua that it wasn't just Moses that was dead—it was a whole old way of doing things that was dead. It died with Moses, and they needed to bury it with him and leave it behind in the wilderness. It was time for something new, and God didn't want Joshua and the Israelites to get stuck in fear after the death of their longtime leader, Moses.

People get stuck after a death, and fear can easily paralyze them. It can be tough to move on, especially into the unknown. We get stuck after major events such as losing a job or a marriage. God knew that He

needed to help Joshua along because now was the time not to be stuck but to arise and go.

Go where? God told Joshua it was time to cross the Jordan River and step into the Promised Land. It wasn't time to be frozen with fear and indecision after the death of their leader; it was finally time to step into the promise with which Moses had carried them out of Egypt and for which they'd been waiting forty years—a land flowing with blessings.

"Every place that the sole of your foot will tread upon I have given you, as I said to Moses," God told Joshua. "No man shall be able to stand before you all the days of your life; as I was with Moses, so I will be with you. I will not leave you nor forsake you" (Joshua 1:3,5, NKJV).

That was an incredible promise, and it wasn't just to Joshua. God has a promise for you, as well, and believe it or not, it's even bigger than that:

Everything we could ever need for life and godliness has already been deposited in us by his divine power. For all this was lavished upon us through the rich experience of knowing him who has called us by name and invited us to come to him through a glorious manifestation of his goodness. As a result of this, he has given you magnificent promises that are beyond all price, so that through the power of these tremendous promises we can experience partnership with the divine nature, by which you have escaped the corrupt desires that are of the world. —2 Peter 1:3-4 (TPT)

I don't know about you, but when I get stuck, I must cling to the promises God has made to me. He's given us His Word, and He has also whispered things to my heart. So when things get difficult, I pull them out to remind myself what He's said. Because, let's admit it; there are times we need God's promises more than others. I feel like now is one of those times.

LET'S ADMIT IT; THERE ARE TIMES WE NEED GOD'S PROMISES MORE THAN OTHERS.

RICHARD PERINCHIEF

I think more people may be stuck right now than ever. As I write this, we're two years into a global crisis. We've seen trouble as a nation before—facing down the Axis Powers in WWII and the shortages at home that went along with the war effort; other wars that divided our nation; deadly terrorist attacks that threatened to bring America to our knees like it brought down the Twin Towers; the Dot Com Bust and the Great Recession that cost so many people jobs and stability.

To that, we can add COVID-19 and quarantines and masks and shots, with people and politics highly polarized. And it is entirely realistic to say that there will be something else a year from now or a decade from now that will make us feel stuck as individuals and as a people. Stuck has happened before, and it's going to happen again.

At our church in Florida, the economic meltdown of 2008 and 2009 hit our people and us hard. We felt it in Florida first because our entire economy was based on new construction and real estate. Just fifteen miles south of our church is The Villages of Lady Lake, the largest retirement community in the world. Over eighty thousand people live there across three counties, and they have built twenty houses a week for twenty years. But when gas prices started to go up in 2007, we felt the first tremor of what was to come. Then, boom! Suddenly, none were selling. Prices were in freefall. Foreclosures hit. They'd had 175 realtors on staff, not counting the independent ones, and several were in our church. One guy I know went from making big six figures to delivering pizza. Those were hard years, and I guarantee that many people felt incredibly stuck and had no idea what they would do.

The COVID-19 pandemic has had its unique issues. Interestingly, I noticed people not returning to work, even as help wanted signs are up everywhere. The Western world, so used to working long hours and sometimes sacrificing families to make money and keep up with costs (and the Joneses), discovered during the quarantine that maybe climbing the corporate ladder or making more money wasn't the be-all

and end-all. We stayed home with our kids, walked our dogs, and were forced to stop and take a deep breath.

And, guess what? People realized that the world spun on.

What if some of the things we thought were so important aren't actually as important as family and time for the simple things? What if the work we're doing isn't as vital as we were led to believe? People all across our country are asking these questions, some for the first time.

The COVID-19 crisis completely changed the job market. The more people worked from home, the more they realized how important family time at home was and is. As a result, large numbers of people are experiencing deep dissatisfaction with jobs that have no clear mission. Without purpose, money is meaningless. Whatever they had been selling or producing or talking about on the phone no longer seemed important, and they don't see the purpose anymore because it doesn't excite them or stir their passion. The opposite is true; they've seen how important it is to spend time with their kids because that other stuff just no longer satisfies.

They realize that there's more to life than making money, and they find that they can be happy with less. That's momentous—we may be seeing a powerful new phenomenon. Now, this can go to excess, but for now, let's look at this as a correction since both parents began working in the decades following WWII.

At the same time, people are hesitating or afraid to return to work. Other factors have been changing as well. When we all went home, many to work, we lost those work/life boundaries. Working from home left us without the distinctions between home and work. Those blurred lines have resulted in more than one awkward video call featuring clothes that are definitely not "business casual" or the embarrassing things kids say at home.

How do you have a healthy work/home balance when your work is now at home with you? It's a challenge, and those blurred lines have increased stress for many and opened eyes across the country. Do you need a big, fancy office and all the upkeep when people can work (and sometimes be even more productive) at home? But if this is a new wave, we're also going to have a lot of people feeling stuck at home who miss the change of scenery provided by "going" to work.

> **HOW DO YOU HAVE A HEALTHY WORK/ HOME BALANCE WHEN YOUR WORK IS NOW AT HOME WITH YOU? IT'S A CHALLENGE!**

My point is this: people feel stuck for many different reasons. It's going to happen, so the question then becomes, "What provisions has God made to help us get unstuck?" I believe He has given us a promise, and I think it will offer us a path forward.

Let's go back to Joshua for a moment. Moses was dead, and if you were one of the Israelites, you could be forgiven for thinking that with his death also died a whole era of godly leadership. You might've even been afraid about the future and felt stuck. After all, Moses was one of the chief Jewish Patriarchs—he was a huge deal. Moses led the Israelites out of Egypt. He wrote the first five books of the Bible, called the Torah. He brought back the Ten Commandments. He talked with God as a man speaks to his friend! And now he was dead.

However, Moses also represented the old generation—the ones that God had let die out in the wilderness because while Moses had brought the Israelites out of Egypt, getting the Egypt out of them was more challenging than you might think. So, with Moses' passing, a new opportunity arose for God to move through Joshua. "Now therefore, arise, go." Those were Joshua's marching orders.

STUCK

Right now, you may feel like forces outside your control have you stuck. Whether that's a global pandemic, an economic meltdown, or something far more personal than that, it may seem as though something else has you trapped. But one of the first things I want you to see is that you may also have an *opportunity*.

The people who went home during the pandemic may feel stuck, but they've also had an opportunity to reevaluate their life decisions. If they were just working to keep up with the Joneses, maybe now is the opportunity to change priorities. Maybe spending time with their family is more important; perhaps they don't need to find fulfillment through work that way anymore.

Being stuck is the perfect time to ask yourself some powerful questions.

Sometimes we need these times of feeling stuck and these opportunities for reevaluation because when everything is flowing along, we don't have the time or feel the need to sit down and ask these questions. Feeling stuck, mainly because of something big ending—a lost job, a broken marriage, even a death—can demand that we ask them of the only One who has the answers.

If you're like me, you probably rarely look at an owner's manual—unless something goes wrong. Then, when your item is working as it should, you stay at your breakneck pace; but when something goes wrong, you're forced to sit down to find out *what* is wrong.

> **[GOD] KNOWS WE'RE MORE LIKELY TO TURN TO HIM WHEN WE'RE IN TROUBLE, AND LIKE A GOOD FATHER, HE IS WAITING FOR YOU WHEN YOU'RE READY TO ASK HIM SOME BIG QUESTIONS.**

Now, it's important to note—I'm not saying God caused a tragedy so that you'd pay attention to Him. But He knows human nature. He knows we're more likely to turn to Him when we're in trouble, and like a good Father, He is waiting for you when you're ready to ask Him some big questions.

- Why am I here?
- Why did you make me?
- Why did you make me like this?
- What am I supposed to do?
- What am I supposed to do now?

But here is one of the most critical questions of all: Are you willing to surrender to the opportunity before you so that God can speak into your life, just as He did to Joshua? Let's face it—feeling stuck is going to either make you shut down even more out of frustration and anger, or it's going to drive you to God, where He can open you up to new possibilities, just as He did with Joshua and Israel.

"Now therefore, arise, go" preceded Israel taking the Promised Land. Moses died first before they stepped into their destiny. Think about that—arguably, Israel's greatest leader had to die before they could enter their greatest blessing.

What has to end for you before you can step into God's promise for you? And what "dead Moseses" are you hanging onto that are keeping you stuck in the wilderness when God's greatest desire is for you to enter the blessing of the Promised Land?

I believe God has something unique and powerful for you, but you must be willing to leave behind what is holding you back to step into the passion and desires of your heart that He has planned and prepared for you. You are more than a conqueror, but conquerors are at their best with something to defeat. You can overcome, but overcoming requires something to get over. You are going to rise up, so what will you step over?

Inside you is a power and a passion because the very God of the Universe lives within you, and He is not passive. Just the opposite.

#

He is passionate! And He is urging you to do something powerful by accepting that your feeling of being stuck means He is also always present with you with an opportunity.

Nothing attacks feeling stuck, like taking action, testing a belief, or gaining a passion. If you are stuck, that means you are in a perfect position to have an encounter with God that will fundamentally change your life! He isn't stuck. He's never stuck! And He is holding out His hand and saying, "Now therefore, arise, go," and leading you to take a step across the Jordan River and into the Promised Land He has for you.

Sometimes taking a step can seem very intimidating. Your fear can keep you stuck. You may remember the story of the twelve spies that entered the Promised Land. Long before Moses died and God commanded Joshua to get up and go into it, Moses sent twelve men in to check out the place God had prepared for them.

Two of the spies—Joshua and Caleb—came back sure God could deliver this rich and prosperous land to Israel. However, the other ten had a different report. The ten reported that the land would devour anyone who went to live there, that the people were huge—giants!—and that the spies felt like grasshoppers in their own eyes.

That fear-filled report shook Israel so much; they counted it truer than God's promise to give them the land. And they proceeded to stay stuck in the desert, wandering, for forty years!

It's easy to criticize Israel for its lack of faith and trust in God, but honestly, I've been stuck because of fear plenty of times. For example, in 1992, our church hit a big financial dip. We were about two and a half years into our ministry, but now we'd had two or three months dropping financially, and we were in trouble.

The pastor of the large church I had trained under had an interesting take on problems—if your church had an issue, you looked for the "sin in the camp." This thinking was probably inspired by an Old Testament story where one man's sin threatened all of Israel. So, this pastor would look for someone on staff who may have been "in sin," . . . and then he'd fire them.

However, as we prayed and fasted about our financial problem at our church, God didn't point out any sin we needed to get rid of. Thankfully, no one was having an affair or cheating on their taxes. We were stuck. So, I brought in a trusted friend as a consultant.

My friend John did a financial audit, talked to staff members, and prayed together with us. He finally came back to share his results.

"I found the problem," he told me.

I replied, "That's fantastic! What is it?"

"It's you." My good friend told me that *I* was the problem. I eventually managed to ask him what he meant. "Well, when's the last time you had a raise?"

"I'm not in the way," I shot back. "What do you mean a raise? I didn't come here for money! I'm not in ministry for that! I'm here to serve God!"

He let me rant for a while, calmly weathering it as I defended myself. "See, that's it! It's almost like *your church is a champagne bottle all shaken up, and you're the cork*. You're never going to ask for a raise, and you don't have a structure in place where anyone is overseeing your pay to give you a raise. So you're setting yourself up to despise your own ministry in a few years."

I could hardly believe what I was hearing. He went on, "I've prayed about this. I think your answer is that you and your associate pastor need $100 a week raises immediately."

I looked at him like he was crazy. We were in the middle of a financial drought, and he was telling me to give myself a *raise*?

"I'd love a raise," I told him, "But we don't have any money."

"I'm so sure this is God," John replied, "that if your finances don't change in two or three weeks, then this wasn't God, and you can go back to what you were doing because I totally missed it."

I reluctantly agreed. And the finances recovered that *very next week* and didn't have another drop for five or six years. So, I asked John to be on my advisory board for the church!

When Gail and I started serving God as pastors, we thought of ourselves as a package deal. *We* were the pastor. She helped with the church, but we had never thought that she should get paid for what she did. So when John found out that Gail didn't get paid, a few years later, he had a similar reaction.

"Does Gail work for the church part-time?" he asked.

"It's closer to full-time," I told him.

"But she doesn't get paid?" he asked. I told him we were a package deal. "This is not good," he told me. "You're not a package deal."

When we were full of youthful zeal and passion, we had told God that if He took care of our bills, we'd even work for free. Money wasn't an issue for us; we weren't looking for it. We didn't want it to get a grip on us and lead to problems as has happened in so many ministries. Yet you need it to live, and we'd lived quite frugally for years in order to go from insurance to serving God as pastors. In fact, there was part of us that was proud of the fact that we *weren't* in it for the money!

"If you don't start paying Gail," John told me, "I will quit the board."

We paid Gail!

Years later, Gail and I look back at those steps, which seemed scary at the time, and we thank God for that wisdom. Our kids love God and are serving the Lord, and I think that if we hadn't listened to John, we would've set them up to resent God and ministry. How many pastors give so much to the church that they have nothing left for their families? We were saved from that.

HOW MANY PASTORS GIVE SO MUCH TO THE CHURCH THAT THEY HAVE NOTHING LEFT FOR THEIR FAMILIES?

RICHARD PERINCHIEF

We were afraid to take both of these steps at the time, but I can now see how they set us free in the long run. Having a board help determine raises for my staff and me freed us to serve God without money becoming an issue either way—greed for too much of it or pride that we didn't focus on it. And by taking the steps my advisor offered, I feel like we set a good example for our children and gave them a better home life.

There were times in some of our dark moments in the Great Recession when things were so onerous that we wanted to go back on those decisions. The pressure was heavy on us both, but hardest of all, I could see the toll it was taking on my wife emotionally. We'd be lying in bed, and I'd say, "Honey, I wish I could fire you."

"Oh, say it again," she'd reply. "That's the most romantic thing you could say to me right now!" She'd run her fingers through my hair as we lay there. Okay, this is a slight exaggeration, but not by much. Some moments in life are more difficult than others. This was one of the hardest we'd experienced up to that time.

We are all called to minister. Not everyone is called to pastoral ministry. But for those of us who are, it's a calling, not a job. You can't really quit! (The Bible says the gifts and callings of God are irrevocable.)

Fear will keep you stuck. However, God understands this, and He offers us a promise to go along with the first step of our recovery from being stuck: "Arise, go. . . . As I was with Moses, so I will be with you. I will not leave you nor forsake you" (Joshua 1:2 and 5, NKJV).

When you feel stuck, your first step may be just a small thing. Perhaps it's just getting up. A friend of mine attended a program he describes as an emotional ER. In it, they give people a description of what the trainers see is holding them back. For my friend, one issue they accurately identified was over-analyzing but failing to do something. From that, he took away a simple idea: When he found himself stuck because of paralysis from analysis, he determined to pick a single, small thing he could do right then. That one little step may not have solved the whole issue, but that's not what he needed. He needed to get off high-center and get moving, and by just picking a small step forward, he found that he could get himself started.

You can't steer a parked car. It locks the steering up. Try to turn the car all you want while it's stopped, and it'll do you no good. You've got to get it moving! You can direct a moving vehicle, even if it's only crawling along.

Does fear have you paralyzed, unable to move? Perhaps something ended for you, and you're afraid of what tomorrow holds. Your "Moses" is dead.

Now what?

I urge you to do the same things God told Joshua: arise and go. Take a small step. It almost doesn't matter what it is; just step out. Make that phone call, handle the apology, write down a couple of things the Lord may be speaking to your heart to do. *Activate* the faith inside you with practical steps toward freedom.

God offers you the same promise from Joshua 1:5 (NKJV). It's far better than a guarantee of your success: "As I was with Moses, so I will be with you. I will not leave you nor forsake you."

Just read that again, and try to wrap your mind around exactly what God is giving us with this promise—He is with us. No matter what, He never leaves our sides. And our promise is even greater than Joshua's because God isn't just with us "as He was with Moses." God is now with us as He was with *Jesus*!

There is nothing you can do to make Him love you more or less, and His presence no longer rests on someone and then leaves. But, if you are in Jesus, you have His Holy Spirit living on the inside of you! He never leaves you hanging, never makes you face it alone.

No matter what you fear, your Father is unafraid. He isn't stuck and never will be, and He's calling you out from among the land of the stuck and into the promises He has for you. You may not understand the *why* behind the next step He's calling you to, just like I didn't understand we needed a raise to remove the cork holding back our ministry, but it's time for your first small step.

God is ready to do something new in you. Are you?

When Moses died in the wilderness, it signaled a new era for Israel. God had done things one way with Moses, but He was about to do something new. Under Moses, God had parted the Red Sea when Moses raised up his staff. Mighty winds came, and the waters parted so the people could cross on dry land.

Under Joshua, God parted the Jordan River, the gateway to the Promised Land, a different way. The priests were to carry the Ark of the Covenant before the people, and God promised that when their feet touched the water, the water would open up.

It wasn't the same. It was new. And, frankly, if I were those priests and I was staring at the quick-flowing Jordan, I might've questioned God's new methods. This wasn't how He'd done it before. What if He didn't come through this time? How often do we think just this way when God is trying to do something new? The Red Sea was the gateway to the wilderness and four decades of wandering. The Jordan was the gateway to the Promised Land, which was metaphorically flowing with milk and honey, yet knowing what we do about Israel (and humans in general), I bet they doubted.

This is exactly why you need to get to know the Holy Spirit. God does things in new and different ways, so you need to know the One who reveals God's next step to you.

When I started learning about the Holy Spirit and how He moves and how He moves in us, I learned that prophetic words, messages, or even conversations frequently give us the next piece of what God is doing. God expects us to take that next step, just like the priests walking into the Jordan River, and then He'll give us the next piece.

It's like that with every word of prophecy I've ever received and shared. If you're waiting to get the whole thing before saying what God is telling you, you might be waiting a long time. For me, God gives me

one phrase or one sentence at a time. The first time I ever prophesied publicly, I was so scared because all I had was this one phrase. But then as I stepped out into that and said what God had given me to say in that moment, He provided the next phrase.

IF YOU NEVER TAKE THAT FIRST STEP, WHO KNOWS IF YOU'LL GET A SECOND?

If you never take that first step, who knows if you'll get a second?

Often, when we're looking for the will of God, we're after the whole plan. We want to know every detail to be sure He's got it all thought out before we move, but that isn't God's MO. He wants you to do the next thing you know to do, and then He'll give you the next detail.

Many people I meet are stuck in indecision, waiting to hear the big picture from God before they step out. They don't know all of what to do, so they do nothing. And, guess what? They tend to stay stuck. If you'll actually do the next thing you know to do, God will open up the way before you as you step forward. Remember, you can't steer that parked car.

Oftentimes, God asks something of us that feels like a risk. I guarantee it felt like a risk to the priests carrying the Ark of the Covenant into the river. But many times, when you're suffering in an area, God will bring someone across your path who is suffering in a similar way. If you'll step out and minister to their need first, suddenly something opens up for Him to meet your need. I've seen that happen over and over again.

Fear can keep you from stepping out or giving in this way, keeping you stuck. It's easy to get into a victim mentality when you're stuck. *Poor me*, we think. *Does anyone see me? I'm stuck here and having a problem.*

RICHARD PERINCHIEF

Can anyone help me? But when we're focused only on ourselves, we can miss the moment where God wants to bring us alongside someone else. Read what Paul wrote to the church in Corinth:

All praises belong to the God and Father of our Lord Jesus Christ. For he is the Father of tender mercy and the God of endless comfort. He always comes alongside us to comfort us in every suffering so that we can come alongside those who are in any painful trial. We can bring them this same comfort that God has poured out upon us. —2 Corinthians 1:3-4 (TPT)

Isn't this powerful? When you are suffering, God's promise to you is endless comfort. He *always* comes alongside us, but just as with being a dispenser of hope, we are also called to be a source of comfort.

When I speak with people going through depression, I urge them to *do something*. Yes, you can go for a walk or get out of the house; those things may help you. However, there is something incredibly powerful about helping someone else when you are struggling. When depressed, a friend of mine says he will often send a text message to someone God may put on his heart. "Hey, how are you?" Good or bad, their response gets his mind off himself and his own struggles.

Gail loves to make what she calls comfort baskets. If you ever come to stay with us in our home, there will likely be one on your bed, but she has them ready for anyone she hears about who's going through a hard time, whether they go to our church or not. The time she puts into making the basket is therapeutic to her, but nothing beats going out and giving someone these little gifts that say, "I'm thinking about you. I care. I hope you feel better!"

If you're stuck, I've advocated that you take *a* step—just one. A small step in *a* direction, even if it's not the perfect solution or something that ends all your troubles. We're talking about a single action, and if you're frustrated and down about being stuck, that step may be reaching out to someone else.

Will helping someone else fix your issue? Possibly, but probably not. However, it may make a difference for them. And don't discount

STUCK

this: Sometimes when you pray, God changes your circumstances. More often, though, God doesn't change your circumstances— He changes *you*.

I want you to take a moment right now to consider the area in which you feel stuck. It might be personal, professional, or spiritual. Pray and ask God for one small thing you can do right now, today. You're not after a whole solution or a big plan—you just need one step. Don't overthink this, and don't sit and wait to hear an audible voice from God or the "Hallelujah Chorus" from a choir of angels.

You're a child of God, and He's put His Spirit in you. All you need is a single move forward.

It's time to get up. It's time to take a step. Moses is dead, and while that scares you, it's okay because God will always be with you. So, leave your dead Moseses behind, and take your first step into God's promise for you today!

CHAPTER 3

THE LIES HOLD US BACK

Sometimes when I hear people talk about God, it seems as though they're making Him a category of their lives, but He doesn't really get out of that corner. I'm not trying to speak negatively about their commitment to God, but years ago I began to learn that God wasn't just one compartmentalized part of my life (even if He came first) but that I want Him first in *all* the various areas of my life—home life, work life, and spiritual life.

I call this a kingdom view because God is not just a priority on Sundays, He is in all of it, my whole worldview. My connection with God when I am at home with my family is as important as it is in business dealings as it is in church and my personal times with Him. In my grandchildren's homeschool, they point out that God is at the center of all the subjects, from math to history, and that we want God to be the center of our lives in every aspect.

I bring this up because I want you to embrace a view of getting unstuck that invites God into *all* the parts of your life because the big idea here is that we are seeking connection with Him.

God knew that He could not just be the top priority of one part of my life but needed to be at the center of all of it. I wanted everything

He had for me, and I believe that this gave Him the room to work in my life, preparing me for what would give me freedom. However, a lie was holding me back from experiencing this. I believe the same thing may be true for you—that as you give Him room to work in your life, He will reveal more of His plan for you. Here's how it happened for me.

I shared with you how God helped free me from one of the biggest "stuck" places of my life when I went forward at the healing service and the pastor prophesied over me as I sat on the floor. Part of me wishes that I had gone to a service like that earlier because we all want to be stuck as short a time as possible. It's *going* to happen, but at least we can minimize that time, right?

Well, maybe. The fact is, I'm not sure I was ready earlier than that. In fact, I think God was at work in my heart, positioning me so that I could even receive His answer to my problems.

> **I KNOW YOU'RE READY TO BE UNSTUCK RIGHT NOW, BUT . . . GOD MAY NEED TO BEGIN A PROCESS IN YOU.**

I know you're ready to be unstuck right now, but I need to bring something up: even though you may feel ready, God may need to begin a process in you. We want Him to wave a magic God wand over our problems and—poof!—all fixed. However, the whole point of this book is that getting unstuck isn't a single step. It's actually a relationship with God, and the by-product of knowing how to connect with Him will help you get unstuck, again and again.

So I told you about the healing service, but I need to tell you what came *before* it that set me up to receive it. In the summer of 1986, I felt the call of God on my life, but I didn't yet know what form it would take, so I was as engaged with my local church as I could be.

That summer, I was asked to teach a youth Sunday school class, and they gave me the Presbyterian curriculum on why the gifts of the Holy Spirit are not for today. I didn't have a problem with it at that point because I didn't know anything different myself.

However, have you ever told a teenager that they should stay away from something . . . and it made them want to check it out even *more*? Well, that may not have been the effect on the kids to which I was teaching this snoozer. But that's the effect it had on *me*!

Surely, there had to be something more to it than they were saying. If all the spiritual gifts had ceased with the apostles (and Paul), why did 1 Corinthians 14 tell me we are supposed to desire spiritual gifts?

I thought I was stuck at that time because I wanted to know if I should follow the call of God on my life and be a pastor or if I should work in insurance and just give. But God knew something else was stuck in me—I was stuck spiritually because the way I knew to connect with God had seemingly taken me as far as it could.

Yet I was hungry for something more. I eventually simply asked God in prayer, "Is there something more?"

And that's when one of the greatest miracles of my life happened. Literally, the pages of my Bible blew open as though a wind had come through the room! I checked the ceiling fan—not on. The window wasn't open, and the AC or heater wasn't on. There was not a single logical explanation for what happened. So, naturally, I looked at where it had blown open.

As I looked at my Bible, my eyes were drawn to Mark 16:17 (NKJV): "And these signs will follow those who believe: In My name they will cast out demons; they will speak with new tongues." As I read this, it became what's called a *rhema* word in my heart—it went from being true in the Bible to being true in my experience and in my life.

STUCK

After I read this, the same thing happened again—the pages of my Bible actually moved! This time, it was John 14:12 (NKJV): "Most assuredly, I say to you, he who believes in Me, the works that I do he will do also; and greater works than these he will do because I go to My Father." I wondered how—how could we do greater works than Jesus?

When I asked my pastor about these passages a few weeks later, he said that Mark 16 is not in every one of the original texts, and Mark is the only gospel this passage is in. He didn't really have a good explanation, but he told me, "It's kind of questionable, and we can't be sure of the authenticity."

I replied to my pastor, "Aren't you the one who taught me that God is sovereign and powerful enough to protect the integrity of His own Word?"

"Well, yes," he replied hesitantly. He had no explanation for that because his concept of God could not include what this scripture was plainly telling me.

Now, I am not telling you all of this because I'm trying to tear down a denomination or a set of beliefs. But I am telling you that my concept of God as it was then was not sufficient to get me unstuck and to where I needed to be. I needed a deeper understanding of God and His Word than my denomination offered.

I wanted more. I didn't even know what I was hungry for, but I knew that the call of God on my life was not getting fulfilled the way I was currently living or under my relationship with God as it was then. And had I gone to that healing service before this divine encounter and those passages, I would likely not have been ready to receive what that pastor prophesied.

This leads me to ask you, how is your concept of God manifested? If you refer to Him as "the Man upstairs" or "the Big Guy" or some cliché statement about God, I want you to think about that for a moment. Is that some culturally acceptable and familiar term that you have actually received into your core beliefs? To me, "the Man upstairs" automatically defines the limitless God of love, joy, and peace as an *old man* waiting to yell at you for being *too loud*! It's a, "Hey, kid, get off my lawn!" kind of *box* we put God into. I can't picture Jesus, who is the expressed image of God Himself, screaming at noisy children and shaking a cane in their faces.

> **I CAN'T PICTURE JESUS, WHO IS THE EXPRESSED IMAGE OF GOD HIMSELF, SCREAMING AT NOISY CHILDREN AND SHAKING A CANE IN THEIR FACES.**

Even though I had never seen something as dramatic as the pages of my Bible blowing around not once but *twice*, I didn't bring it up with my wife right away. I kept quiet because while I was raised Presbyterian, where we thought people who spoke in tongues were weird, she was raised fundamentalist Baptist, who believe those people are demon-possessed!

However, my appetite was whetted now—I was curious, and I was excited because of those verses and how God gave them to me. I keep reading my Bible, looking for passages I'd always discounted before.

One night, my wife took our kids to her parents' house, and I pulled out my Bible and began to read the book of Acts. We'd never read it in my church, and I'd never heard it preached. I devoured the whole thing in maybe two hours, and I was *on fire* in my spirit! I didn't find anything in there that backed up the Sunday school curriculum they'd given me for those teens; nothing said things of the Spirit had ceased. I couldn't find a part where it said that it had all ended with the twelve apostles plus Paul.

So when Gail got home, I said, "We need to talk." I needed to tell her what God was showing me.

To my surprise, she said, "Yeah, we've got to talk."

"Okay," I replied. "You go first."

She said, "The last few weeks, I've been seeing scriptures I've never seen before."

"Like what?"

She pulled out her Bible and took me to—wait for it—Mark 16 and John 14! The same verses I had read when my Bible blew open!

We had never heard a Pentecostal or charismatic preacher. Yet God is so good that He had been speaking to both of us, showing us His Word separately but at the same time (even though neither of us knew it).

We became detectives, reading our Bibles and looking for what the Word of God itself—not the churches we were from—had to say. Gail went even further. When I was away working, she began watching Pat Robertson's show, *The 700 Club*, and other things on Christian TV.

As we began hearing testimonies about healings and other miracles, we began to grow in conviction: these were the "greater things" Jesus had mentioned in John 14!

Yet even then, as our spirits were coming alive with excitement, we didn't say anything to our friends, though it was very difficult. Our church had been so afraid of charismatics that when we joined it in 1982, we'd signed a document that said that if the subject of the charismatic renewal ever came up, we'd quietly leave the church and not cause division. God impressed on us that we needed to honor that. However, instead of operating independently, now we were hungry for more of God *together*. God had always spoken to both of us a bit like that, but He had taken it to a new level!

The night of Halloween 1986, we were watching Christian television, and the preacher was talking about powerless Christians. He could preach! My wife was lying at the end of the bed as we watched, and I was propped up on a pillow.

As he looked at the camera, the preacher's message cut us to the core. He said that if we felt like we were powerless Christians, we needed to be filled with the Holy Spirit. "I don't care what you're doing or where you are," he said, "reach out and grab somebody's hand. I'm going to pray for you right now!"

I took my wife's hand, and when he prayed, it felt like *electricity* hit us right where our hands were joined and shot out of us! It was so dramatic, and we were so excited when we realized that both of us felt it at the same time, that we jumped up off the bed shouting, "It's real! It's real!"

And, suddenly because we'd signed that document at our church, we realized that though we wanted to share this incredible experience, we couldn't tell our friends about this amazing thing that was happening in us. In fact, we quickly saw that we couldn't even go back to our church.

It was time for something new.

I love telling the story of how God spoke to me through that preacher and answered my question because I had felt so stuck for so long that getting an answer like that changed my life completely. However, if God had not laid the groundwork in the months before, I'm not sure what the results may have been.

God wants to set you free of whatever is holding you back. Whatever reasons you have for feeling stuck, He has a plan for your life—one that He longs to reveal to your heart. But He needs you to be ready! If a great rainstorm falls in the desert, the ground cannot absorb it because it's too dry. It just washes away. God does not want that to happen in your life; He wants to prepare the ground of your heart to receive the seed He's planting in you so that your life will yield a great harvest.

GOD WANTS TO PREPARE THE GROUND OF YOUR HEART TO RECEIVE THE SEED HE'S PLANTING IN YOU SO THAT YOUR LIFE WILL YIELD A GREAT HARVEST.

You see, I wasn't just ready to learn what God had for me—insurance or ministry—I was hungry for the change in my heart that would make that ministry *possible*. Without first receiving the Holy Spirit, I was not able or ready to be the pastor God was calling me to be. He needed to do that work first.

You want to get unstuck, but what work does God need to do in your life *first*? It's time to begin asking yourself what *God* thinks is necessary before you can move from being stuck. He knows what you need, and He has equipped you for every good work. But there may be something He needs to develop and grow within you to get you ready and able to do those good works. So right now, I want to encourage you to put this book down for a few moments, grab a notebook, and seriously ask Him this question: "God what do You want to do in my life now?"

Spend some time seeking Him in prayer. Then, come back, so I can tell you the next part of our story because we weren't done with the obstacles yet—and neither are you. However, whatever is holding you back (like fear!) doesn't stand a chance against the power of God!

God wasn't done with us, and I wasn't done with Him, either. I was hungry for whatever He had next. It turns out, that was receiving a personal prayer language, tongues—but it wouldn't happen the way we expected.

Perhaps a month after Gail and I had our electric experience while holding hands and praying, I was out on my insurance route and talking to one of my clients. She was a dynamic and insightful woman, and she could see something on me right away.

"What's going on with you?" she asked.

"What do you mean?" I asked. She asked me if I were in the ministry, and I told her, "No, but I am going after God."

"Have you been baptized in the Holy Spirit?" she asked. I told her I had, and then she asked, "Well, do you speak in tongues?"

"No, ma'am," I replied. "But I'm hungry! I want to know if it's real. I want everything God has for me!"

She smiled really big. "I'll bring a couple of sisters from our church and come to your house," she told me. "We'll bring some anointing oil. We'll lay hands on you, and we'll get you speaking in tongues!"

"Yes!" I agreed. Now, I just had to tell my wife.

What I didn't know was that back at home, one of my wife's friends had come over. She had felt something was up with us, but Gail's experience was very different than mine. Her friend had brought over a pamphlet called *The Corinthian Catastrophe*—a little book against the gifts of the Spirit by a guy who used to be Assemblies of God and then renounced it all.

I was ready to invite the sisters over to our house to lay hands on us, and Gail met me at the door saying, "I've got some questions for you!"

We proceeded to have an enormous *disagreement*. Don't be fooled; just because God wants you unstuck and growing in your connection with Him, it isn't necessarily going to be easy. We often have to overcome opposition, and that is with good reason. Just like you can't help a baby bird emerge from its shell, God cannot take shortcuts with your development. Without resistance, the baby bird doesn't get the experience it needs to live a healthy life. Without resistance, you don't build muscle when working out. Without resistance, you wouldn't grow in some way that God has determined is vital for your next steps. But, I know—it's hard!

To me, our experiences are a great example of spiritual warfare. My client could tell something was different about me and could smell the move of God on my life. The same was true for our other friend. But something very different was motivating her to bring that little booklet than was motivating the woman who wanted to pray for us to receive the gift of tongues.

The result was division. I wanted everything God had for me, but after reading that pamphlet, Gail was frightened. "I don't care if it's God," she told me, "I don't want it!"

STUCK

We went to bed at odds. I didn't know what to do, but that night I felt so drained I went to bed early, which was unusual for me. I didn't know what to pray, so I just whispered, "God, get her!" With that, I drifted off to sleep. . . . only to wake up hours later as Gail shook me because God had been moving on her powerfully!

My aunt had already told us about the preacher we went to visit, and my wife had recorded his show. I hadn't seen it, but Gail ended up watching it after I went to bed. His message was on prayerless saints, and though she didn't know it yet, Gail was a prayer warrior!

When Gail came to wake me up, she was speaking in tongues so fast I called it machine-gun tongues! She hit me to wake me up, and I sprang out of bed shouting, "It's real! It's real!"

It took a while to calm her down and get the story out of her. When she had finished watching the recording, she said it hit her really hard about her prayer life. She told me that she had gotten on the floor and prayed, "God, I don't mean to be stubborn about this stuff—I really do want the whole thing. I'm just afraid of this tongues business." She had heard so much teaching against it, but she wanted the real thing.

She told me that God began reminding her of sins and things that she had thought she'd dealt with—not in a condemning way, but to show her how He had cleared this and that from her life. Though we didn't know the wording at the time, I now would call it a loving pathway to deliverance. God was meeting her where she was and dealing with what was holding her back.

It was time to get unstuck.

IT WAS TIME TO GET UNSTUCK.

As Gail was getting ready for bed after that time in prayer, she began to sing this little Baptist tune. "He is able to carry me through!" she softly sang. As she brushed her teeth, she couldn't stop singing. As she got changed, she couldn't stop singing. As she lay down, she still couldn't stop!

She didn't want to stop and was trying to be quiet when suddenly her prayer language rose up within her, and she began to speak in unknown tongues, just as they had in Acts. This blew my mind, and it defied everything I understood about how God works. I had gone to bed telling God I wanted everything He had for me. Gail hadn't wanted it, but *she* got it? How was that fair? But, I must admit, I *did* pray for God to do this!

My aunt had told us that back in the '60s and '70s, during the charismatic renewal, that if someone was having trouble getting their prayer language, they'd have them say the word "hallelujah" backwards three times fast. So I tried that. "Hallelujah," I said, but no matter how fast or how much I bungled it up, I was just saying "hallelujah" backwards.

Then I remembered something else. "See if you can do it again," I told Gail. We'd also heard that sometimes people laid hands on others to receive their prayer language, so as she began to pray in tongues again, I grabbed her hand and put it on my head. As she prayed—*bang*!—my prayer language released in exactly the same way Gail's had only about an hour after she received hers.

God knew that He needed to show these two Christians a full experience because with our background and the churches and doctrines we were from, nothing but a gusher of an experience would work. We needed to see a dramatic move of God, and that's exactly what He did to bring us into the full experience He wanted us to have.

Fear had held us stuck—fear of the things of the Spirit. We'd heard so much teaching and so many things that just weren't correct or biblical, created by other fearful people, that God had to soften the ground of our hearts so that we could receive the new move He wanted to do.

What holds you back, dear reader? Is it fear? Gail confessed she was afraid that she might just start spontaneously speaking in tongues

in the grocery store because we'd received false teaching and didn't understand that Scripture plainly explains that the spirit of the prophet is subject to the person's will. Because the people who say the gifts of the Spirit have ended stop reading at 1 Corinthians 13, we'd never read 1 Corinthians 14:32 (NLT), which says, "Remember that people who prophesy are in control of their spirit and can take turns." That fear of bursting out in tongues in the grocery store was founded on a lie that the Word of God answered.

To get unstuck, you will need to let go of the things that are holding you back. For us, it was fear and incorrect doctrine. For you it may be something different.

We were stuck at least in part because other people had pushed things on us. That may be your experience as well. However, as well as they could present their doctrine that the gifts of the Spirit had ceased, when Gail and I began looking in God's Word for the answers *ourselves*, God was faithful to show us the way.

You may not have the pages of your Bible blow open or find that God has separately been whispering the truth to you and your spouse, but He has a pathway forward for you that is in agreement with the Word. God will never tell you to do something that is not in line with the Bible—the whole Bible, not just a passage taken out of context, as they'd done with the incorrect doctrine we'd learned. God cannot oppose His Word because *Jesus is the Word!*

Even though God is in it, your freedom will probably not come without a fight. Gail and I experienced spiritual warfare for our breakthrough. What are the odds that our friend would come over with that booklet at such a pivotal point at the same time my client was offering to pray for us? God was moving, but the enemy was buffeting us with his waves at the same time.

RICHARD PERINCHIEF

EVEN THOUGH GOD IS IN IT, YOUR FREEDOM WILL PROBABLY NOT COME WITHOUT A FIGHT.

The enemy doesn't want you free. He has a plan for stealing your future, killing your hope, and destroying your life. But, if you are in Christ, the enemy has no power over you! He has no authority, and he has no right to you!

What he can do is lie, and he does it very well. He'll seek to convince you that you're no good, that there's no hope, and that you will always be stuck.

Gail and I had believed a lie that the gifts of the Holy Spirit had ceased. But God knew that our freedom required us learning the truth: that these things are for now, and that we can experience the full measure of His miracle-working power today.

It was the key that allowed me to receive my answer to the question of whether I was to be a businessman or a pastor.

What lie are you believing? What have you believed about yourself, about God, about others that's holding you back from experiencing the freedom you hunger for? God is a God of freedom.

Jesus proclaimed Himself to be the fulfillment of this prophecy from Isaiah:

"The Spirit of the Lord is upon me, and he has anointed me to be hope for the poor, healing for the brokenhearted, and new eyes for the blind, and to preach to prisoners, 'You are set free!' I have come to share the message of Jubilee, for the time of God's great acceptance has begun." —Luke 4:18 (TPT)

Are you ready for all He has for you?

CHAPTER 4

YOUR BURNING BUSH MOMENT

God has something great for you, but as I learned when my friend John helped us in the early days of our ministry, sometimes we are the problem—the cork in the bottle. Our stuck can even hold back others around us, as I was at my church, and at the root of it was my pride . . . in my humility. The Word tells us that God resists the proud but gives grace to the humble, and my pride—I was proud because I wasn't in it for the money—was holding me and my church back. Plus, it had positioned me for *God* to resist us. As a result, in a few years, I was positioned for my own ministry to become a stumbling block to me—an issue that would trip me up and cause resentment. If I didn't get my heart right, I'd end up resenting my own ministry.

You see, I had to get out of my own way and quit stopping the flow. The Holy Spirit flows out of us like a river of living water, but we can stop up that flow. In Israel, they have the Dead Sea, a body of water that has no outlet. There is no flow. It's dead because there's no outflow, so it stagnated and has become so salty, it's not suitable for drinking and is actually poison to whatever tries. In contrast, a river has a *flow*

to it—a beginning and an end. It has a headwater where it starts and a delta where it ends.

The river of living water within us, the Holy Spirit, has a flow as well, and just as a river has a mouth, so, too, do we. Ours can get us in plenty of trouble! With our mouths, we say words that can trap us and keep us stuck. I've certainly been there. I've also tried to help others who are there, and I've learned something important. You can throw someone a line to help them get free, but if they keep themselves stuck with their mouths, it will almost never work. We get in our own way, and we can create a downward spiral with our mouths.

> **I CAN'T GET YOU UNSTUCK—ONLY YOU CAN DO THAT. ONLY YOU CAN GRAB ONTO LIFELINES PEOPLE THROW YOU.**

I can't get you unstuck—only you can do that. Only you can grab onto lifelines people throw you. Even God will not overrule your will; that's why He gave it to you and why it means so much when we choose to love and follow Him.

To put it another way, your will can be keeping you stuck. Sure, you say that you want to get free, but I said that when our church was stuck financially, too. I wanted to move forward badly, but until the issue of my will was addressed, I was the cork in the bottle—me.

Maybe you've been praying about whatever has you stuck. You may have even been praying for *years*. If you want some perspective, go back and read Abraham's story and how long he waited for God to fulfill His promise. I guarantee that Abraham felt pretty stuck—for *decades*.

I've had such promising people in my church who ended up not being able to get out of their own way—people I've thought could grow into pastors. And I've seen some of them limit or even destroy themselves with their words and their self-assessments. Others got a little taste of authority, and it seemed they couldn't handle it. I've talked and prayed with these people many times, but while I feel like we had the rescue rope thrown out to them, some have been unwilling to take it and make the internal changes that would free them as the cork in the bottle. These aren't people living immoral lives; these are just people who couldn't get out of their own way.

Some get stuck repeatedly in slow downward spirals. They get a little spark of opportunity or excitement for a brief moment but seem to sabotage their own success with delusions of grandeur (over-the-top, unattainable goals beyond anything they've actually been asked to accomplish), setting themselves up for one disappointment after another.

So how do we get out of our own way? Part of the answer lies within the thought of simplicity. One of the pastors who speaks into my life always says, "Simplify to strengthen!" In other words, when you want to get something stronger, you have to begin with removing the clutter that's all around it. When my wife and I have done some home renovation, we start with cleaning out or removing all the stuff we don't use, don't wear anymore, or don't really need. While redecorating a room, my wife loves to start with a clean canvas by imagining everything *gone*.

Our lives can feel so busy and full and toxic. To move forward again, to get out of our own way, we have to get back to the basics. Set priorities and boundaries. Get God back in the center of your life, the throne of your heart. Seek first the kingdom of God, and all these things (you need) will be added to you (see Matthew 6:33). Life works best when God is first!

One of the biggest things that I have seen hold us back is comparison. It's endemic in our culture; it's at the core of almost all advertising and nearly all social media—it's everywhere. I have nothing against social media, but the temptation is always there to compare your real life, with all its warts, to someone else's best moments and filtered photos. The

problem with comparing yourself to others is that you'll always find someone doing more than you or having more than you, and you'll get jealous and envious. Then again, you can also always find someone doing less or having less, and you'll get prideful. Either way, you lose!

> **YOU'LL ALWAYS FIND SOMEONE DOING OR HAVING MORE THAN YOU, AND YOU'LL GET JEALOUS AND ENVIOUS. THEN AGAIN, YOU CAN ALSO ALWAYS FIND SOMEONE DOING OR HAVING LESS, AND YOU'LL GET PRIDEFUL. EITHER WAY, YOU LOSE!**

It's easy to fall into the comparison trap when you're viewing someone else's seemingly perfect family or vacation or new house or car. Studies show that it can make us depressed, anxious, isolated, and afraid we're missing out. According to an article in *Business Standard*: "Facebook, Twitter, and other social media users regard themselves as unhappier and less popular than their friends, a study has found."[1]

I may be focusing on social media here because it is so apparent. As a society, we're discovering more and more research identifying how the comparison trap ensnares us as we allow it. Comparison can grab us whenever we compare ourselves with others, and it's been a problem for a long time.

Paul wrote, "We do not dare to classify or compare ourselves with some who commend themselves. When they measure themselves by themselves and compare themselves with themselves, they are not wise" (2 Corinthians 10:12, NIV). Unfortunately, when we compare,

---

[1] Press Trust of India, "Social Media Makes People Feel Unhappy, Less Popular: Study," *Business Standard*, 27 Nov. 2019, https://www.business-standard.com/article/beyond-business/social-media-makes-people-feel-unhappy-less-popular-study-117062200799_1.html.

we're using others as our standard of measurement, and it will always feed our insecurities.

Insecurity is at the heart of comparison, and it will always make it worse. To one level or another, we all feel insecure. When we compare, we're just feeding it. Try complimenting someone. When the person deflects it, it's often not modesty; it's insecurity. You may say someone looks nice, and they'll reply, "What, this old thing?" Or they'll point out they got it on sale. Others swell with pride right in front of your eyes. Rarely is someone secure enough to just accept the compliment with a "Thank you." Why? Because we're reacting out of our insecurities.

And how can we not feel insecure if we're judging ourselves based on other people's highlights on social media, the constant pull for more in the advertising, or looking at perfect people from Hollywood who spend untold dollars on plastic surgery, personal chefs, and airbrush artists? If you're judging yourself based on *People* magazine, you're going to feel inadequate and shabby. Yet, how often are those peoples' lives falling apart as they bounce from marriage to marriage and rehab to rehab?

Most people who make us feel inadequate are just projecting an image that isn't real anyway. Our whole system of comparison is based on a lie.

The Bible tells us we are to have no other gods before Him, but how often do we make what we think is true of another person an idol in our lives? We dream of that star's influence, that friend's perfect family, or that acquaintance's nice car or house. We hold that up as the standard, the thing we desire. But Hollywood is fake, and most people are broken inside. That perfect family only looks perfect because they took seventeen pictures to get that "perfect" one, and that acquaintance may have sacrificed everything else to get those nice possessions.

Comparison gets you stuck because it's a trap, and it's doubly dangerous because you're not even comparing yourself to the truth—you're comparing to a crafted, created image that others want you to see.

Just look at how a music star's image changes, such as girls from the Disney Channel. When they reach their middle or late teens, someone whispers in their ears that it's time to leave the little kid thing behind to become sexy. Seemingly overnight, they transform from wholesome little girls into sexualized symbols of what someone thinks an attractive, desirable woman should look like. Britney Spears, Lindsay Lohan, Miley Cyrus—the list goes on and on, and look at the lives they step into as they try to transform themselves into what they think (or are told) is appealing. The worst part is some of these young performers were squeaky-clean, professed Christians. By reports, Katy Perry was a tongue-talking, Spirit-filled believer—and today she's this woke image of a secular pop star.

Is that who you want your children to become? If comparison is a habit you hand them, that's whom they're going to look up to and want to emulate.

You can always find someone who is prettier than you, younger than you, richer than you, or more successful than you—and the opposite is true as well. When we compare, it creates an identity crisis because the only one we're supposed to look to is Jesus, who is our role model. So what do we do? How do we get out of the trap?

The apostle Paul told us that it's foolish to measure ourselves by ourselves (or others), but the truth is that there is only One who is good (see Romans 3:10). There is only One whose standards mean anything, and He has already followed up actions with words by sending His only beloved Son, Jesus. This is because God knows you are so valuable. He gave all He had and allowed Jesus to die on a cross because you're worth it. When you know where your genuine esteem comes from, you can be comfortable in your own skin and with who you are.

You don't have to make yourself into someone who is acceptable; you already are.

RICHARD PERINCHIEF

YOU DON'T HAVE TO MAKE YOURSELF INTO SOMEONE WHO IS ACCEPTABLE; YOU ALREADY ARE.

God has a history of using those who struggle with insecurity, and Moses may be one of the best examples. After being raised in Pharaoh's household for forty years, thinking he'd deliver Israel on his own and killing an Egyptian, Moses fled into the wilderness—where he lived for another forty years. By the time God appeared to him in the form of a burning bush, Moses had gone from prince to shepherd. Can you imagine the hit on his self-esteem?

As God laid out His plan for Moses, this broken man replied, "Who am I that I should go to Pharaoh and bring the Israelites out of Egypt?" (Exodus 3:11, NIV). Objection after objection, the Lord worked with Moses:

But Moses pleaded with the Lord, "O Lord, I'm not very good with words. I never have been, and I'm not now, even though you have spoken to me. I get tongue-tied, and my words get tangled." —Exodus 4:10 (NLT)

In everyday language, Moses stuttered. God was sending a man with an insecure view of himself, who had been broken down significantly, to speak to the most powerful man in the world—and Moses was a stutterer. Moses even begged the Lord to send someone else, but God knew what Moses needed and had a plan for his life.

Have you ever felt like this? I guarantee that Moses felt stuck out in that desert, tending his father-in-law's stupid sheep. He probably felt stuck by his broken confidence, his shattered self-image. But listen to how God answered Moses—not about what Moses could do, but what God would do through him:

Then the Lord asked Moses, "Who makes a person's mouth? Who decides whether people speak or do not speak, hear or do not hear, see or do not

see? Is it not I, the Lord? Now go! I will be with you as you speak, and I will instruct you in what to say." —Exodus 4:11-12 (NLT)

God will always answer your insecurity with His ability. In other words, God actually wants to build your confidence in His expertise and capability. There is nothing too hard for Him.

I believe it is vital that we all have our own burning bush moment—our own encounter with God—if we want to move Him from a subject to be learned about to a person we encounter personally. God is not a cosmic force or even a standoffish deity with unknowable plots for your life. He is a good, good Father, and He can be met and known intimately.

In fact, if you genuinely want to get unstuck, there is no other way than to get to know this amazing God as waymaker, the One who blazes new trails right before your eyes and opens up what has been closed off to us.

Look at Moses and his brokenness, but understand this—he grew up under the Egyptian system for forty years, learning its ways. He had everything money could buy and was part of the royal family. And while it took forty years to get Egypt into his system, it took forty years for God to get Egypt out of Moses. (That proved true of all of Israel—it took forty years to get Egypt out of them, so they could be free of the slave mentality that bound them.) Moses was stuck in a mentality of privilege, and by the time God could use him, he seemed to be a broken shell of his former self. If Moses still compared his current life to his former life, he would've been unable to be the man God called him to be. Moses had to let all that go, and when he was broken, God could finally do something with him.

Notice that God met Moses exactly where he was, chasing sheep around in the middle of the wilderness. It took something as dramatic as a burning bush to snap Moses out of it and begin showing him how God saw him, rather than Moses comparing his current life to that of a prince of Egypt. Moses needed a burning bush, and I needed a feeling like electricity coursing through me when Gail and I were filled with the Spirit—God knew He'd need to do something dramatic to get our attention and show us He was real, to break us out of the stuck we were in.

What would you like Him to do in your life?

Gideon is one of my favorite guys from the Old Testament. Talk about insecurity! When we meet Gideon in the book of Judges, he was hiding, threshing wheat down in a winepress. To me, that's an image of his dysfunction as a person.

> **IT'S EASY TO GET COMFORTABLE IN OUR DYSFUNCTION; WE GET USED TO IT.**

It's easy to get comfortable in our dysfunction; we get used to it. It's a silly example, I know, but it makes me think of a toilet we had in our house. It didn't work right for years, but it would flush if you jiggled the handle just right. Instead of fixing it or getting someone out to repair it, we just got used to it. That's what we do with our insecurity and our dysfunction—we don't fix them; we learn to live with them. It takes God coming along and saying, "You don't have to live like this," to change us.

Listen to how God greeted Gideon as he hid in his winepress: "The Lord is with you, mighty warrior" (Judges 6:12, NIV). I guarantee Gideon didn't feel like a mighty man of valor! On the contrary, I assure you he felt stuck, frustrated, afraid, and insecure. And, you know what, God didn't berate him! He didn't criticize Gideon for hiding in the winepress. No, He called out the person He saw inside Gideon.

It's a measure of Gideon's dysfunction that he didn't just nod and go along with God; he objected and questioned and asked for sign after sign. At no point did God shoot him down for this. "Why are we going through all this if you're God?" Gideon questioned. "Why are we suffering? Why don't we see miracles anymore?"

STUCK

Have you ever felt like this? Like you expected to see God in a certain way, but then He doesn't do that, and you get discouraged? Do you get disappointed? Eventually, that happens enough, and you doubt it will ever be something different. You're stuck.

Yet what was God's answer to Gideon? Just as it was to Moses: "The Lord is with you." "I am sending you." "I will be with you." (Judges 6:12,14, and 16, NIV).

It's His answer to you as well: "I am with you." This is your burning bush moment—not the flash and the fire, but the fact that God promises to be with His people over and over again, fulfilled in Jesus Christ who isn't just with you but in you.

John the Baptist, who was Jesus's cousin and preached of His appearing, eventually found himself in prison. He sent his disciples to Jesus because he couldn't go himself, and he asked a big question: "Are you the Messiah we've been expecting, or should we keep looking for someone else?" (Matthew 11:3, NLT) Can you believe that John, who seemed so convinced that Jesus was the Christ, who saw the Holy Spirit descend on Him like a dove at His baptism, asked that question? I can—because John was human, just like you and me.

Jesus answered John's question and insecurity with the only answer that mattered—Himself:

> *"Go back to John and tell him what you have heard and seen—the blind see, the lame walk, those with leprosy are cured, the deaf hear, the dead are raised to life, and the Good News is being preached to the poor."* — *Matthew 11:4-5 (NLT)*

This was the man of whom Jesus said no one greater had ever lived, and he had doubts and questions. John wrestled with insecurity, and he was definitely stuck in prison.

Yet God's answer to him (and to you) isn't to point to you—to your shortcomings or how you compare to those around you. He points to Himself. He reassures us by directing us back to Himself and Who He is in us.

Do you want to break the comparison trap? Do you want to be free from its power? Don't focus on what others are doing. Focus on Jesus. Everything in the Old Testament, the Law, and the Prophets pointed to Jesus, and He did all He told John's disciples—and more. He gave you Himself so that you, yes, you, could do even greater works than those.

People who know God is with them, is in them, need to compare themselves to no man. God has judged you, and He has found you worthy because of Jesus. He is with you, and He will never abandon you. He loves you so much that He put you in Jesus and Jesus in you so that you would never be inadequate again. You may have questions and feel stuck from time to time, but you have within you everything you need to be set free as often as necessary.

> **GOD HAS JUDGED YOU, AND HE HAS FOUND YOU WORTHY BECAUSE OF JESUS.**

Gideon questioned repeatedly, asking for sign after sign that God was with him. Over and over, the Lord proved Himself, and eventually, when the chips were down, Gideon received his answer so clearly that he sent most of his army away. All of Israel was stuck, and because one broken, damaged, and dysfunctional man could learn to believe God was with him, their enemies destroyed themselves.

What enemies does God want to destroy in your life? Comparison? Doubt? Fear? Insecurity? Perhaps it's addiction or emotional scarring. Maybe it's your false ideas about Him. Whatever the stronghold is, you possess the mighty weapons necessary, by the power of the Holy Spirit, to pull it down and teach it to obey the knowledge of Him.

God is with you.

CHAPTER 5

SHOW YOUR SCARS

When we get stuck, all we want is to get out of being uncomfortable. We don't like it, and it's scary. Maybe you picked up this book intending to simply get out of whatever you've been in, and that's fine. It's obviously part of the goal to learn how to get unstuck, both now and next time. But before we go any further, I want to mention something that may help you.

There can be a purpose to your stuck—and it may go beyond you.

I'm not going to disrespect your pain and claim that it's all for a higher purpose, and you should be glad you're so uncomfortable. But neither will I hand you some magic formula for getting unstuck if you'll just quote these three verses while standing on your head. Frankly, we don't have that kind of control.

The reality is that freedom isn't a formula; it's a relationship with a Person. And though it's not always comforting in the moment, He doesn't waste anything, and He will even use your experiences of being stuck. So let's dive into that together just a little deeper for a few moments.

In the last chapter, we saw that Gideon learned, as Joshua had before him, that one of the first steps in getting unstuck for any of us is knowing that God is with us. The beauty of it is that God never seems to tire of reassuring us. Gideon put out his fleeces and asked for other signs, but

he was far from the only one in the Bible to need reassurance of God's presence and love. I hope that comforts you a little because I don't know about you, but I need confirmation from time to time—okay, often!

Many things may get us stuck, but we stay stuck as Christians because we doubt God's presence with us and goodness to us. When we cannot trust Him, we often have trouble accepting His gifts—some of the very things that set us free. So what do we do with these doubts? First, let me tell you that doubting isn't as bad as you think. And second, God is familiar with dealing with those of us who have doubts, and He has a plan to help you grow in your ability to trust Him.

> **GOD IS FAMILIAR WITH DEALING WITH THOSE OF US WHO HAVE DOUBTS, AND HE HAS A PLAN TO HELP YOU GROW IN YOUR ABILITY TO TRUST HIM.**

You may have heard the term "doubting Thomas," referring to Thomas after Jesus's death and resurrection. The first time Jesus appeared to the disciples, Thomas wasn't there with them, and he said that he'd believe when he could see it. Sometimes I think we've given Thomas a bad rap, acting as though we'd do it differently if we were in his shoes.

However, the way Jesus handled Thomas should tell us a lot. The second time Jesus appeared to His disciples, He immediately went to Thomas. He didn't say, "I dub thee 'Doubting Thomas,'" and condemn him. That's what religion does. Instead, Jesus came to him and showed Thomas His scars. "Put your finger here; see my hands. Reach out your hand and put it into my side. Stop doubting and believe" (John 20:27, NIV).

I say this to help answer a difficult question: if we're saved and set free, why does God let us get stuck? And what do we do about it? To me, at least part of the answer is that we may actually want the scars of what we've been through someday. I know that sounds bizarre, but bear with me for a moment because understanding this requires a kingdom perspective.

God wants you to reach people who won't be able to just listen to your pretty little victory testimony. If you've lived a charmed life of nothing but ease and blessing, it won't win over the hearts of those who have been through life like hell on earth. Those people need to see something else—your scars, the evidence that you've come through a lot yourself.

Many people will come to know God not because they see how blessed you've been but because of the scars which are proof of what God has brought you through. Your scars are like street cred to them; they're evidence that you've been through some serious stuff, but you came out the other side. They want to see that you've been through something like they've been through, that you understand their pain and trials. To them, your scars are evidence that you've been through something and conquered it—that God has brought you through. And if God got you through your hard times, it's reassuring to them that He can bring them through hard times.

To me, these people aren't doubting Thomases about whom we should feel negative; they're precious people who need to see proof that God is who He says He is, does what He says He'll do, and will do it again even when things are difficult.

You may like to know that I've been to the area of India where Thomas went some two thousand years ago. In a country dominated by Hinduism and a myriad of other beliefs, there are Christians today who trace their background of faith back to "doubting Thomas" and the missionary journey he took there so many years ago.

In the gospel of John, there's a story so controversial that it nearly broke the system. It's that of the woman caught in the act of adultery (question: where was the man?). The religious leaders brought her before Jesus in an attempt to trap Him into saying something they could

use against Him. This tells me that they were, in a twisted way, already learning what Jesus was about and were trying to use it against Him.

But Jesus was simply too wise for them. Instead of answering, He bent down and began to write in the dirt. While many have tried to guess what He wrote, we ultimately don't know. What we do know is that when He stood up, He said this: "All right, but let the one who has never sinned throw the first stone!" (John 8:7, NLT). What an answer!

Then we read, "When the accusers heard this, they slipped away one by one, beginning with the oldest, until only Jesus was left in the middle of the crowd with the woman" (John 8:9, NLT). I believe that these older guys were the first to recognize their sin, and because of their life experiences, even these jaded manipulators began to have a little compassion. They dropped their rocks, and I think we must do that too.

Partly because of the churches we were involved in after we received the baptism of the Holy Spirit, I thought that signs and wonders, miracles and healings, were the main ways of showing the world how much they need Jesus. I still believe this is true, but I feel like God added another dimension to it as well. The greatest things that bring people to God are when we drop our rocks and show our scars instead. People who are stuck need to see us vulnerable. They don't just want to hear your victory reports and how you got unstuck; they want to see what you've been through, that you're human, and you've been there yourself. Your knowledge of God's power to set people free isn't just theological; it's experiential. Because you've had an encounter with the God of the universe, and He is with you, you can now show others that He brings His people through over and over.

> **BECAUSE YOU'VE HAD AN ENCOUNTER WITH THE GOD OF THE UNIVERSE, AND HE IS WITH YOU, YOU CAN NOW SHOW OTHERS THAT HE BRINGS HIS PEOPLE THROUGH OVER AND OVER.**

As a person who has been through hard times and seen God's faithfulness, you're in a powerful position to drop your rocks and show your scars. The scars you bear from the times God has gotten you unstuck may be the very things that help bring others to know Him. They can be God's way of redeeming the difficult times you've been through while giving them purpose beyond your own life. Our freedom is directly connected to trusting God, and our faith gets boosted when we look back at what He's done in the past. That can also be a key to helping others get free as well.

You see, your freedom isn't just for you.

Earlier, I said that the path to getting unstuck isn't a simple formula—it's a Person. I want to revisit this because if there's anything I want you to take away from this book, it's that He is the solution and that He is with you. My hope for you is that you form a solid pathway to Him as you read this.

For me, that path led me to the floor with a notebook, learning to hear God as He told me that we'd find a place with new carpet and new paint. To get unstuck, I've had to find a way to connect with the person of Jesus Christ and have an encounter with Him, and I want you to find your path to joining with Him as well. For me, I was flat on the ground, writing what He told me. For you, it might be in a coffee shop or out in nature. The point isn't how you do it; it's Whom you connect with and that you trust Him to release you when you're held captive. I don't want you to copy my methods; I want you to copy my destination—Jesus! God will meet you where you are when you reach out to Him.

It's vital to know Him and trust Him because you're not always going to see or understand the path He has laid out for your next steps. That's certainly been true for us. When we moved to Orlando to go to the thriving church there, we felt like we were leaving Egypt and heading to the Promised Land. We were finally free! God delivered us and set us on a path to knowing Him at ever deeper levels.

And then, after I'd only been on staff at the church as an actual ordained pastor for about two years, the path took a turn. To our dismay, we felt God was leading us to move and start a church—back in Ocala! Having brought us to the Promised Land, was God now sending us back to Egypt?

I needed to tell you the story about Thomas and how God wants to use our scars because as we argued with Him in prayer, we began to understand that God was sending us back so that we could be instrumental in setting others free. It's like He was saying, "Now, go back to Egypt and set My people free!"

No! We didn't want to go. We liked the big church we were in, and it was just exploding at that time. Talk about insecurity! I didn't feel like I was "that guy," the head pastor—and if I were, I didn't feel ready yet. (Let me just tell you this: You will almost never feel prepared to take the steps God will call you to that will be instrumental in setting you or others free. After all, if you felt ready, what would you need Him for? Yet just as with Gideon, God will always provide confirmation.)

> **YOU WILL ALMOST NEVER FEEL PREPARED TO TAKE THE STEPS GOD WILL CALL YOU TO THAT WILL BE INSTRUMENTAL IN SETTING YOU OR OTHERS FREE.**

After Gail and I had prayed about this prompting for a while, I eventually told my pastor, "We feel like we are supposed to go back to Ocala and start a church."

He smiled at me. "I always knew you would go back to start a church. How soon can you go?" I thought we might go in a year or two, but here he was asking me how soon I could go. We started less than a month after I shared my vision with him! And God was so good, providing for us every step of the way. Our pastor was gracious enough to keep me on the payroll for a few months, keeping us on the church's health insurance, and sending us off with his blessing. Not only that, the church provided us with office furniture and other things.

It wasn't until we were driving behind the U-Haul truck with all our stuff in it, moving back to Ocala, that it really sank in. We had just resigned from one of the most prominent up-and-coming churches in America to move back to the place where we had once felt so stuck and from which we felt like God had set us free by moving to Orlando. It was both surreal and terrifying at the same time.

The pieces began to fall into place with a location to meet and even a few people who came during our first four weeks. Honestly, it was a time of sheer terror, wondering if we had done the right thing. However, Gail was so strong and reassuring, reminding me that God was with us and that we both had felt this call to move. Not only that, God had confirmed His word to us through multiple sources, including our pastor.

We needed to hold onto that because our first year was challenging. I don't want to get into the details, but it was a trying time in which we needed lots of reassurance from the Lord. In fact, what followed were some of the most painful feelings of being stuck that I've ever experienced. I didn't know it, but it was time to make some scars.

People came to the church, and people left. Some we thought that we could trust ended up betraying that trust. It got so bad that a group of dissatisfied former churchgoers came into the church building where we were meeting and began ripping stuff off the walls and taking all the technical equipment and wiring, wreaking havoc on the building. We were left with no chairs in an empty building with no sound equipment, completely broke and broken inside, both in our hearts and in the actual building itself.

However, God was with us even then. We had roughly one-fourth of the church sign up for a mission trip, confirming one of the great

passions and purposes that God gave our hearts. And as we made a shopping list of furniture and equipment for which we had no money, a complete stranger stopped by one day. "I just felt like I was supposed to come here because God told me to give you guys $1,000," he said. That $1,000 felt more like a million to my faith.

In those moments of pain, I came very close to quitting. I was completely dependent on God, my connection to Him my only lifeline. I remember praying, "God, if You're with me, if You're in this church thing right now, it's imperative that You show up because I'm at the end."

And it was right there in my painful moment that God did indeed show up.

The mission trip, which was to Trinidad and Tobago, was already planned, so we went, despite all the difficulties. While we were there, God gave us another reassurance. A prophetic woman, trusted by men I knew, had a word for us. God shared through her that there had been termites in the foundation and that He could not build on what we had without first clearing them out. "I have removed all the termites, and now you can arise and build," she shared from the Lord.

Remember our scripture from Joshua?

"Moses My servant is dead. Now therefore, arise, go over this Jordan, you and all this people, to the land which I am giving to them—the children of Israel. . . . As I was with Moses, so I will be with you. I will not leave you nor forsake you." —Joshua 1:2 and 5 (NKJV)

The old had to pass away before we could step into the new. The people who had come with us on that mission trip became a termite-free foundation on which the Lord could build. We were reassured that God would always be with us, and within three weeks, we had brand-new chairs instead of our dilapidated old ones. We had a brand-new sound system instead of the old buggy setup. We had brand-new nursery equipment that was better than the stuff we had before, yet I bear very real scars from those months starting our church. It was a near-death experience for me, spiritually.

RICHARD PERINCHIEF

GOD WASN'T DONE.

But God wasn't done.

The man who was instrumental in causing so much trouble and taking many people to another church didn't experience much success with that. In fact, that church closed, but later, he started another church for older people which is still thriving today.

We occasionally encountered each other over the years, and I admit that I did not handle some of those meetings well. But it wasn't until roughly twenty-five years later that God brought it full circle and ministered final healing. Gail and I ended up sitting behind this pastor and his wife at a conference, and I felt this nudge from God (we will talk more about this in a future chapter) to say something to him.

I went up to him and said, "I owe you an apology." He looked at me, surprised, and began to tear up.

"You don't owe me anything," he said.

"Yes, I do," I told him. "When you tried to make peace, I was really smug about it, and I've regretted it for many years because I didn't receive you. You were trying to do a good thing, and I acted like a jerk."

"All is forgiven," he told me. "I just want you to know that I'm happy for your success. I'm not against you; I'm for you."

Honestly, I was shaken by this encounter. With tears in my eyes, I pulled together the team of people I had at that conference and told them, "These are great ideas, but now I know that our next season of growth is coming because God just allowed that." Many of them knew the story, and some had even been there.

It was a cathartic moment of healing, and it was amazing how God brought it full circle. I believe in full-circle moments, especially in our relationships and wounds. I've experienced many of them, and it is

valuable to know that the damages we incur one moment can become the scars that point to a great and amazing God down the line.

God wants you unstuck, but it isn't just for you, and it certainly isn't just for your convenience. It is not His purpose to torture you, tempt you, or bring you problems maliciously and then call it character building. Unfortunately, we live in a fallen world where bad things happen, and we can often feel trapped and hostage to those moments. But I want you to know that God can create purpose in your pain. A day will come when you will look back and see all that He's done for you, and it will encourage you in a new time of difficulty. Not only that, He can bring great meaning and significance to others through your scars, pointing the way to His goodness and mercy and His ability to bring you through even the most difficult and trying of circumstances. You may be stuck right now and only want to get free, but God has far more in mind than simply getting you unstuck.

He wants a relationship with you, a connection with you. He wants you to turn to Him every time you get stuck, struggle, and have problems. I firmly believe that a day will come when the point will no longer be that you got out of a difficult situation. Still, He will use the scars you bear to show another the way to connect with His Son, so they, too, can enjoy incredible freedom and a relationship with Jesus Christ.

> **GOD WILL USE THE SCARS YOU BEAR TO SHOW ANOTHER THE WAY TO CONNECT WITH HIS SON, SO THEY, TOO, CAN ENJOY INCREDIBLE FREEDOM AND A RELATIONSHIP WITH JESUS CHRIST.**

How would you feel if God used your freedom to help someone else find theirs?

CHAPTER 6

GENERATIONS OF FREEDOM

When I was a senior in high school, I walked into my sixth-period class, looking for an easy grade as I'd already completed my required classes. This was our first day, and the teacher told us to turn our desks around to find two people closest to us for a discussion. I did as I was told—and was face-to-face with Gail Patrick. She and her best friend were sitting next to each other, so we formed a little group and began the discussion.

It immediately struck me that Gail was full of compassion. She was already a Christian, and while I had been raised in church all my life, I didn't know Jesus. I believed in God, but I had not had a personal encounter with Jesus Christ—not because people in my life hadn't told me to call on the name of Jesus, but despite the head knowledge, I didn't know Him, and I was not paying attention to Him.

Now, I was dating another girl at the time, but as I talked with Gail, I had this amazing spark with her! Within a few weeks, we were really hitting it off. Around the same time, I found out that I had been nominated for something called senior calendar. The people who raised the most money would get their picture taken to be in the senior calendar, and I was surprised to be one of the nominees.

STUCK

"What are you going to do to raise money?" Gail asked me. I told her that I had just found out I was nominated and had no idea.

"I guess some people have done bake sales. Can you bake anything?" I asked her.

She smiled. "I make really good chocolate chip cookies."

Oh, man, I was hooked. I'm an absolute sucker for chocolate chip cookies—in fact, I've been known to vacation and search for the best chocolate chip cookies—only to find they're at home, right where they've always been!

> **I'VE BEEN KNOWN TO VACATION AND SEARCH FOR THE BEST CHOCOLATE CHIP COOKIES—ONLY TO FIND THEY'RE AT HOME, RIGHT WHERE THEY'VE ALWAYS BEEN!**

Gail asked a few of her friends for help, and we all met at her house. I was impressed; this seventeen-year-old girl made the most amazing chocolate chip cookies with no recipe. The next day, they all sold out! I told Gail that we needed more cookies, but that night none of the other girls showed up—just her. So, there we were, making chocolate chip cookies at my house for our very first date!

Gail and I dated all through our senior year of high school, and we were very serious. It was young love, but honestly, we fought like cats and dogs, and I was a terrible boyfriend. She would threaten to break up with me if we fought, and we actually broke up for probably the tenth time as we both went to college.

We still saw each other occasionally, and in that first year of college, I was quite the party guy. So we continued to get together and break up again. It was December 31, 1979, and we were leaving the '70s and entering the '80s. That night I went to see her and then went to party with my friends. When I finally dragged myself home, I had the most vivid dream. I usually don't remember my dreams when I wake up, but this time I remembered vividly.

A godlike voice spoke to me and said, "Your girlfriend is pregnant. If you marry her and give Me your life, you'll have a son, a family, and I will do great things with your life."

I still wasn't saved, but I'd grown up in the Presbyterian church, and I kind of took this seriously. I called Gail the next day and told her I'd had the weirdest dream. "Well, I'm not pregnant," she told me. "Did you go party with your friends last night?" I had; I hadn't gotten home 'till five in the morning. "So it was probably a party dream," she concluded.

That was New Year's Day, 1980, but a few weeks later, she called me. "I'm late for my cycle, and I think I might be pregnant." I hadn't thought about the dream since, but suddenly it all came back. I took her that Saturday to get a free pregnancy test—at an abortion clinic. I was the only guy in the room; the rest were girls with their mothers or alone. The place had a darkness to it, as though it were the beginning of a funeral for all these babies.

Gail went in for an exam, and when she came out, she was crying. Gail hugged me and told me, "Yeah, I'm pregnant." I told the nurses how young we were and needed some counseling, so a woman came in and started putting out brochures.

"Well, what I can tell you is that abortion is safer than having a baby. Having a baby is very dangerous, especially for a young woman who is just eighteen," she told us. Then, she began laying out all the reasons we should get an abortion, but she refused to tell us details about the procedure. "I can't tell you much more than that it is safer," she told us. "But I can tell you how to raise the money without your parents knowing."

That was her counsel—abortions are safer; get the money without your parents knowing! Wow! I felt like she was handling us as though we were cattle, but this was a life-or-death moment.

"So, do you want to have the abortion?" the nurse asked. In tears, Gail nodded; she would have the procedure. Just then, another lady came in to tell us they'd already done the last abortion that day. We'd have to come back Monday or Tuesday. We went home with paperwork and instructions about what kind of clothing she should wear when we came back.

We walked out of the door into this weird moment of life. We knew that it wasn't right, but we'd signed up for it anyway, and we ended up going to breakfast at Burger King. She was starving, but Gail found that for the first time, she couldn't eat a thing.

Suddenly I said, "Remember that dream I had?" I asked, "What if that was God?" She had me remind her about the dream, and it all came back in vivid detail—that a voice told me that she was pregnant but that if I would marry her and give Him my life, we'd have a son. It gave us a stark contrast from how the woman at the abortion clinic had spoken about a fetus, not a baby. In fact, she wouldn't say the word "baby."

I told Gail, "If that was God—if there's even a remote chance that it was really God—then that's our son, not just tissue. I want to get married. I want to marry you!" We'd talked about getting married; we'd been together for over a year and a half by this point. We had talked about getting married after we graduated, but here we were, just two scared teenagers in a wild, surreal moment. It was almost like watching a movie.

We decided right there, sitting in Burger King, that we would not get an abortion. Instead, we would get married and keep our baby. However, we were not going to tell her parents yet! I wanted to talk to my dad first because I knew that he would know what to do. Gail's family was involved in a challenging time, so we would lean on my father and his advice.

Thankfully, I had a great relationship with my dad. When I got home, he was mowing the yard, so I sat down on the diving board and waited for him to notice me. I was keenly aware that these were the final moments of my youth and that as soon as I told him this, I had to grow up. Once I told him, everything would change, and I wouldn't be able to go back.

> **ONCE I TOLD HIM, EVERYTHING WOULD CHANGE, AND I WOULDN'T BE ABLE TO GO BACK.**

He was emotional about it when I told him, but he also said he totally supported me. We decided not to tell my mom quite yet, or anyone else because I was going to ask Gail's parents for her hand in marriage and try to do things honorably. So we didn't want to tell anyone about the pregnancy.

When we told Gail's parents, her tough-guy dad was crying—not what I anticipated at all. I expected my amazing saint of a mother-in-law to weep and for him to want to kill me, but we soon found out that he had gotten married at our age because he had gotten his girlfriend pregnant and had another daughter long before he met Gail's mother. Gail met her half-sister when she was about twelve, and this felt like history repeating itself, as though there were a generational tendency rising up again.

"I think you're too young, but I know you're in love, so I will give you my blessing," her father said.

Oh, and by the way—we're pregnant!

We got married on March 21, 1980. We bought a little brand-new mobile home that turned out to be an easy bake oven with no air conditioning in Florida!

God was just getting started, though. I told Gail I wanted one final crazy night for my bachelor party; I affirmed I would never cheat on

her, but I intended to do everything else like getting drunk and high. I swore to her that it would be the last time, but when a friend of mine who had been out of town for the wedding came back a few weeks later, I went out with him to party against Gail's wishes. I came home with candy and flowers and sheepish shame. She was already in bed and had been crying all day. I begged for her forgiveness.

And it was at that moment, that I realized there would always be "one more time." After that, I couldn't change myself. I thought being a Christian was about being a good person, but this was the first moment I could honestly say I was aware of the whole concept of sin.

> **I REALIZED THAT I WAS STUCK IN MY SINS, AND IT WENT FROM MY HEAD TO MY HEART THAT I COULD NOT CHANGE MYSELF.**

I suddenly realized that I was stuck in my sins, and it went from my head to my heart that I could not change myself. So I knelt by her side in our bed, looked at Gail, and said, "I'm going to pray right now." But I didn't know what to pray. "God, I know you're out there. If this Jesus thing is real, then I need to know You for myself. My aunt told me that I could ask You into my heart, so come in my heart. Help me change because I don't know how."

I was still a smoker at this point, and the following day, the first thing I noticed was that instead of wanting a cigarette, I wanted to read the Bible. Our only Bible was a giant book we put on the coffee table to look like Christians, even though I'd been no more born-again than a seagull. But I felt this gentle nudge, this tap-tap in my heart, to start with the Bible, so before I went to work, I cracked that thing open.

RICHARD PERINCHIEF

My son Ricky now jokes that he led me to God, and what can I say? I didn't go forward to an altar call at a church; I fell on the altar of recognizing I was broken, desperate for God to change me. By the time Ricky was born, I was reading a devotional out of the book of John, and I was really getting into knowing Jesus. My life was forever changed, thanks to a dream that God gave me weeks in advance that saved our son's life. To this day, I have never had another dream or vision where God told me about the future as clearly, but at that moment, God not only saved Ricky's life but He put me on a pathway to knowing Him personally.

It was time to establish a new direction, a new tradition for our family. Gail and I may have gotten married early and under less-than-ideal circumstances, but God had begun a work in us that changed the course of our future. Perhaps you feel stuck right now because of things that happened in your past or your family's history. We were stuck, heading towards a wrong decision, but this is precisely what it took for me to recognize that I was stuck in my sin. God was ready to set me free, but it took this crisis for me to be willing to change my family's future.

Are you ready to change the course of your family's future? You can, even if you're fighting the history or tendencies of your family. Let's look at how.

At the risk of dating this book, I love a series of commercials. They're joking around about how we become our parents. I'm willing to bet that in your own life, you've heard something that sounds like one or both of your parents come out of your mouth—even if you slapped your hand over it right after.

In my circles, there's been a lot of debate over the years about what you might call generational curses. Are they real? Can they impact born-again Christians? Psychologists debate what's called nature vs. nurture—in other words, are we the way we are because of issues like genetics or the environment in which we're raised? I'm not here to try to give a definitive answer to either of these issues, but I'm inclined to believe that most of the debate is semantics. Whatever title you call it,

people can be impacted by issues that span generations because there's obviously plenty of evidence of generational tendencies in families.

> **WHATEVER TITLE YOU CALL IT, PEOPLE CAN BE IMPACTED BY ISSUES THAT SPAN GENERATIONS BECAUSE THERE'S OBVIOUSLY PLENTY OF EVIDENCE OF GENERATIONAL TENDENCIES IN FAMILIES.**

It's funny when we realize that our jokes or the words we use when getting onto our kids sound like our parents, but it's different when you feel like you're stuck . . . just like others in your family have been stuck. Maybe it's an addiction such as alcohol, a history of bad relationship choices, medical problems, or drama and trouble that seem to follow you around. Whatever it may be, our family histories can seem to get us bound up.

The very first thing God reveals about Himself in Genesis is that He is the Creator. The enemy is a counterfeiter, not a creator; he can't make anything. However, the advantage that he has is that he has seen what slipped up your father or grandfather. He knows our human nature and our wiring, and he knows that if he can press certain buttons, he may be able to get the same result. Your bloodline can get you stuck.

Thank God that we have a new bloodline as children of God! Thanks to the blood of Jesus shed for us; we're born into a living hope. If you've never stopped to think about the words "born again," do so now—you have been born anew, separate and distinct from your parents or grandparents because Jesus's spiritual DNA is now in your DNA. That means that whatever your family history, you're not bound to the failings and frailties of your earthly lineage because you are now a child of God if

RICHARD PERINCHIEF

you're in Christ. Another way of looking at it is that you and I were dead in our sins, but Jesus paid that price for us, and God has breathed new life into us. The dead man, with all the hang-ups and vulnerabilities the enemy used, is dead and gone. New life now lives in you!

So why do we still get stuck, even as Christians? It's not because we have a sinful nature anymore; we're dead to sin and alive in Christ. What we have now is a sin habit, and habits are made to be broken.

My full name is Richard Kenneth Perinchief. As I mentioned before, generations of Perinchiefs have been preachers, but at first, I looked like I would break that mold—until God got a hold of my life! I'm kind of named after my grandfather, a Methodist pastor named Kenneth Richards Perinchief. But my dad also had a favorite uncle, also a Richard; we called him Uncle Dick. My parents sometimes said I was named after Uncle Dick which became an issue over time.

Uncle Dick was really frugal. Okay, let's be honest, he was cheap—a notorious, miserly skinflint. He and my Aunt Helen would come down from Pennsylvania to Florida to be with us in the winter for a bit. I remember one time Uncle Dick took us to Morrison's Cafeteria. This place had people who would take your tray and carry it to your table, and you were supposed to put a tip on the tray for them. The problem is, Uncle Dick didn't tip well—he left a dime on the tray for all of our trays! My dad was mortified, so he snuck back in and slipped them a dollar each, and this was back in the '60s when that would've been pretty good.

Now, even as a kid, I was known as what I'd call a clean freak, maybe even what you'd call a germaphobe. I liked it a certain way. I didn't want anyone drinking after me, so I didn't like to share my drinks or anything. I can remember that whenever my friends and I would trade toys, I always got the best deal; I'd come away with a G. I. Joe with real hair, and my friend would leave with an old deck of cards. Over time, as I'd act like that, my parents would say, "You're just like Uncle Dick!" It became like a self-fulfilling prophecy—the more they said it, the more I started to resemble my supposed namesake.

By the time we got married, that tightwad thing was firmly on me. Now, Gail is super generous; at our church, she's in charge of finances for the giving ministries, and she loves to give it away to missions or benevolences. She has a gift of giving. Being married to a tightwad must've driven her crazy!

But the thing is, after God started getting a hold of my life, something began to come out in me. I love to give almost as much as she does! However, I had been locked up and stuck in this generational expectation put on me. It took God reforming me before it began to come out that I was more like my heavenly Father, the ultimate giver, than I was my cheap Uncle Dick. You may remember that before God pointed me toward ministry, it even got to the point that I seriously wondered if my role in the body of Christ would be as a successful businessman and giver.

It takes the Lord to change us; we cannot do it ourselves. No matter how hard you try, you cannot reform the old man within you. He needed to die, and that's exactly what happened when you received Christ. However, we have to participate with what God is doing. I call it getting your second wind.

Scientists debate the exact physiology of how a second wind works, but for our purposes, it is the burst of energy that we get when we push through. I have found in my spiritual life that's part of how I get unstuck—pressing through the challenging moment where I feel like quitting. I tell you all this because if you are persisting through generational tendencies, you will get tired and frustrated. You will feel like you make progress only to get stuck again. You may even wonder if you got enough of a transfusion of the blood of Jesus. But let me assure you that His work on the cross is complete! You are free from your old life of sin, and you have been made into a new creation. However, you will carry negative inertia with you, habits that the Lord must break down and remake into the image of Christ.

You'll face a decision. If you quit, you're going to stay stuck. However, if you push through, it's going to be difficult. Which will you choose?

I often feel like God has told me something, and I take the initial steps to act on that. When the going gets tough, I now know to keep on pushing through because eventually, if I do not give up, God is going to give me confirmation of His word to me.

> **WHEN THE GOING GETS TOUGH, I NOW KNOW TO KEEP ON PUSHING THROUGH BECAUSE EVENTUALLY, IF I DO NOT GIVE UP, GOD IS GOING TO GIVE ME CONFIRMATION OF HIS WORD TO ME.**

Two times in Matthew, Jesus said something powerful. (I hope you know that if it says it once in the Bible, it's important, but if it says it more than once, we should really pay attention!) Jesus said, "He who endures to the end will be saved" (Matthew 10:22 and 24:13, NKJV).

Let me just tell you now and save you some time—if you were expecting to get unstuck by just reading this book or doing something once, you're going to be disappointed. Getting freedom is not something that happens at the snap of your fingers; it is a lifestyle of how to deal with your feelings of being stuck. You must endure. You are learning to connect relationally to the One who sets us free, and you will know to come to God again and again as often as needed every time you find yourself stuck.

Confirmation is God's way of giving me a second wind and encouraging me to keep pushing on. Even on this book, when I shared the vision for it as a guest speaker, the church generously gave to me not just the blessing they usually give; the pastor also asked if the congregation

would like to seed into the writing of this book. With very little information and on no notice, they generously gave toward putting this all together. It was unexpected and unsolicited, yet it was a powerful confirmation from God that I was doing the right thing.

We only get a second wind by pushing through. For example, if you're running and stop to rest, you will not get that second wind. Instead, you are likely to stiffen up (in other words, get even more stuck). The only way you get a second wind is by refusing to quit. You see, physically, we get a second wind when the body acclimates to the oxygen demand of stress, such as from running a marathon. According to science and tech writer Neel Patel, "Second wind is the 'flush of relief' when your muscles finally get the oxygen they need."[2]

We are spiritual beings, initially created when God breathed life into a lump of clay and created Adam. Nothing has changed; we still need the breath of God to live, and His oxygen in our spiritual lungs is what gives us fresh energy to push through and overcome.

Paul puts it like this: "Can anything ever separate us from Christ's love? Does it mean he no longer loves us if we have trouble or calamity, or are persecuted, or hungry, or destitute, or in danger, or threatened with death?" (Romans 8:35, NLT). In other words, if these things happen and you feel stuck, does it mean God doesn't love you? No! Paul goes on to say, "Yet in all these things we are more than conquerors through Him who loved us" (Romans 8:37, NKJV).

You cannot be a conqueror without something to overcome. And you cannot get your second wind, the breath of God, without endurance.

Hebrews speaks of running the race of life:

Therefore, since we are surrounded by such a huge crowd of witnesses to the life of faith, let us strip off every weight that slows us down, especially the sin that so easily trips us up. And let us run with endurance the race God has set before us. —Hebrews 12:1 (NLT)

---

2 Neel V. Patel, "What Causes 'Second Wind' in Runners?" *Inverse*, 3 Nov. 2015, https://www.inverse.com/article/7687-what-causes-second-wind-in-runners.

Great, you may say. But how? "We do this by keeping our eyes on Jesus, the champion who initiates and perfects our faith" (Hebrews 12:2a, NLT).

This is about relationship—our connection with God. And the beauty of it is, He is not a God out of touch with what it's like to be us, to be stuck. Jesus understood it intimately; after all, He once hung on a cross. Yet read how He pushed through, why, and the result:

> Because of the joy awaiting him, he endured the cross, disregarding its shame. Now he is seated in the place of honor beside God's throne. Think of all the hostility he endured from sinful people; then you won't become weary and give up. —Hebrews 12:2-3 (NLT)

> **THIS IS ABOUT RELATIONSHIP—OUR CONNECTION WITH GOD. AND THE BEAUTY OF IT IS, HE IS NOT A GOD OUT OF TOUCH WITH WHAT IT'S LIKE TO BE US, TO BE STUCK. JESUS UNDERSTOOD IT INTIMATELY; AFTER ALL, HE ONCE HUNG ON A CROSS.**

Don't give up! Whatever you're going through, please don't give up. You don't know how close you may be to a breakthrough! What if Joshua had given up when they entered the Promised Land, and it was difficult to drive out the pagan inhabitants? What if the children of Israel had given up on the sixth lap around Jericho? What if Jesus had given up in the garden when He prayed and asked God to let the cup of suffering pass from Him?

Only in pushing through will you get your second wind. Whether you are facing fresh difficulties or tendencies passed down from generation to generation, God has freedom and breakthrough for you that can remodel your life and even change the course of your future.

It may even save a life—perhaps yours!

CHAPTER 7

OUT OF YOUR CONTROL

We've spent a lot of time talking about inner things that can keep us stuck, but sometimes we feel trapped by circumstances outside our control. If you are stuck by something on the inside, you may feel like you have a measure of control. But situations outside of our control can leave us feeling like victims. Sometimes someone else's terrible decision affects your life, and it isn't even remotely your fault. Other times, I even feel stuck geographically, in the wrong place in life. So, what do we do when we are stuck in times like these?

It reminds me of a story in the life of David. He and his men returned to their home base to find that enemies had raided it, destroying the town and taking all of their families prisoner. With their homes burned to the ground and their families captive, things turned south very quickly. Angry with him, David's soldiers begin to talk of stoning him! But one passage of scripture tells you how David handled this circumstance that was outside of his control: "But David strengthened himself in the Lord his God" (1 Samuel 30:6, NKJV).

How did David accomplish this? The Bible doesn't say—and that might be a good thing because this may look different for you than for David or me. It may not even be the same from one circumstance to another. That said, I have found that certain things encourage me in

the Lord. I may find reassurance in the promises of the Bible, especially certain passages I feel like the Lord has given me specifically to hold onto. At other times, I remind myself of words of prophecy that have been spoken over me, such as on our mission trip in the story I told earlier, where the woman had a prophecy that God had needed to give us a new foundation. I'm encouraged by music, and I know that praise and worship that touches the throne of God has often been a resource for me. Godly wisdom from a trusted friend may strengthen us and so might times of intensive prayer.

My point is that finding strength in the Lord is not a formula. There's not a single thing guaranteed to work every time you're stuck. It's not about a system—it's about a Person. It's about God, Himself, not how you get to Him.

> **IT'S NOT ABOUT A SYSTEM—
> IT'S ABOUT A PERSON.**

The world may feel like it is collapsing around you, and I'm sure that's how David felt. But he encouraged himself in the Lord, and after that, David dared to lead his men because God answered him: "Yes, go after them. You will surely recover everything that was taken from you!" (1 Samuel 30:8, NLT).

His connection with God pointed out the next step, and he and his soldiers set off in pursuit. David knew what to do because he'd connected with God.

But don't get the mistaken idea that if you encourage yourself by connecting with God, everything will be easy and perfect. David set out with six hundred men, but they were tired already, and two hundred of them were too tired to keep up the chase. I bet David was tempted to wonder if he would be able to receive God's promise missing one-third of his force, but he pressed on.

They came across a young man, abandoned by his masters and left for dead. After nursing this man back to health, he agreed to guide them to David's enemies. They were able to come upon them by surprise. David and his four hundred men defeated an army, and the Bible tells us, "Nothing was missing: small or great, son or daughter, nor anything else that had been taken. David brought everything back" (1 Samuel 30:20, NLT).

I love this story because it looked so bleak, but by connecting with God, David received a plan to get out of the trap he was in and receive back everything the enemy had stolen. What has the enemy stolen from you? What has being stuck cost you? The list will be as varied as the people who read this book, but I want to assure you that God is moved by the prayers of His people.

You may feel trapped right now by circumstances outside of your control, but it is time to encourage yourself in the Lord and look for how He wants to restore you.

At one point, it seemed as though we had constant financial problems. We prayed about it quite a bit because we were trying to determine the root of the issue. Then, one night, one of our trusted prayer partners, who was a little older and more experienced than we were, had an all-night prayer meeting at his house with us. He had seen us go through these troubling financial times even when I was on staff at the large church in Orlando.

My friend said, "I just can't get away from this. I feel like there are words that have been spoken that are blocking your blessings financially."

"We tithe, we give, and we believe. What else are we supposed to do?" I asked.

He thought for a few moments. "Maybe you should sit down and actually put something in writing, a covenant with God. Find a few scriptures about God's blessing, and make sure you make a fresh

covenant about your financial life with Him. We are going to break those words that have been spoken over you."

God showed us that people in authority in our lives had spoken words over us years ago that somehow impacted us financially. So, at the encouragement of my friend, we wrote down all of the scriptures on blessing and prosperity we could find in every book of the Bible. We wrote them by hand on pieces of paper, and then we wrote a statement to God. We said, "God, we are making a contract with You. We will tithe and give no matter what, and we will be faithful to bless others however You say because this money is Your money. We believe Your Word, what it says, and that it proves that You want to bless us. Therefore, we formally renounce the words other people have spoken over us. We break the power of those words in the authority of Jesus's name!"

We experienced an immediate change financially! We had been held back by words spoken outside of our control, but God wanted something different for us.

Now, I want to tie together a few strands and stories from different points in this book. While things changed right away for us financially after this prayer and our contract with God, the battle wouldn't be complete for a few more years because this area would prove sticky for me again.

We just talked about ways we get stuck generationally. The generational issues we talked about (that I was just like Uncle Dick) came together with words spoken over us—all things we could not control—to create a mentality in me that kept me stuck for years. Unconsciously, after I moved toward ministry, I felt destined to be poor, all for the sake of the Lord. I'd developed a martyr complex; I was proud of my humility, of being poor.

Then, another friend, years later, told me those game-changing words you'll remember: "It's you." I was the problem. I was the cork in the champagne bottle. I learned to become a great giver, but I was a lousy receiver until I completed a mindset change. The fact is that I needed to be both—a giver and a receiver.

As Christians, we major in being recipients of the greatest gift of all time—Jesus' gift of dying on the cross in our place and the eternal life He offers us instead. As receivers, we can then give. I needed to learn to be both if I wanted to leave behind the final remnants of the traps the enemy had laid for my life.

While we didn't have control over the Uncle Dick comparisons or the words spoken over us, God held the solution: I needed to own it and be willing to follow godly counsel on how to change it. I wasn't destined to struggle financially as a pastor, nor should that be a source of pride. I had to let it go if I wanted to be free.

Can you see how all these things come together? Being trapped often isn't just about one of the issues that keep us stuck—it's about layers of causes put down throughout our lives, like sets of chains that hold us bound. You may gain some freedom in an area of your life as God breaks one set of chains, but the work is often not complete in a day or even a year. God wants a life of total freedom for us, and we must engage with Him intimately to feel out each new aspect of freedom He desires and how He wants to accomplish it in our lives.

For me, I had to let go of my pride about being a poor, dedicated pastor to receive what God had for me. I had to remove myself as the cork in the champagne bottle, or I would grow to resent my ministry. My freedom had one other aspect to it as well.

You may remember that before God answered my prayers about whether I should be in ministry or insurance, I had looked for wisdom. One of the people I'd asked for wisdom was a pastor. He'd discouraged me, telling me, "If you can do anything else in life and be satisfied, be something else—don't be a pastor." He tried to talk me out of it.

The Thanksgiving following my friend's prayer that the words spoken over us would be broken, I talked with my father-in-law. He'd come to

work for us at the church as an administrator, and he opened up to tell me something he hadn't shared with us—an issue going back years.

He had talked with that pastor right before we met, and he'd asked him to discourage me from going into ministry because he didn't want to see us live in poverty. "I was the cause of all that," he confessed.

God wanted me free, but this had to be resolved. Remember, it's not about the formula; it's about a relationship. It wasn't enough to just break the words spoken over us. God wanted to restore this aspect of my relationship with my father-in-law.

Instead of being stuck under generational issues and words spoken over us, God had another plan: "Let the elders who rule well be counted worthy of double honor, especially those who labor in the word and doctrine" (1 Timothy 5:17, NKJV). It wasn't time for poverty or being stuck any longer. God was setting us free, and it was instead time for double honor. The cork came free, and our ministry began to flow.

When Gail and I were newly filled with the Spirit, I listened to a tape (this ancient, Stone Age way of recording things) from a preacher speaking in South Africa. As he was talking, I felt something rise up in my heart. I turned the recording off and listened to what I felt God was saying. *You're going to preach to the nations*, I felt like He told me. Later on, I felt like God confirmed that with another word: *You're going to go to at least one hundred countries.* This was in confirmation with what the pastor in Orlando told us after I fell down under the Spirit. I took these words as confirmation that God was calling us to a greater ministry than just something local—but at the time, I wasn't even a preacher yet!

I was still in insurance, and I remember thinking, *But we don't have any money. I think we have a problem.* How would we travel the world without any money? Nevertheless, I told God, "If You want to do that, I'm in."

I had often felt like there was something on me, a gift for traveling. So when I was sixteen, I toured Europe with a friend of mine. Airfare there and back in 1977 was $400, and I had $1,000 in my savings account, so my parents let me go. We spent three weeks with his relatives in Germany and Austria, and for three weeks we used the Eurail Pass and slept on trains, ending up visiting thirteen countries. I loved seeing Scandinavia and going all the way down to Italy; it was one of my most incredible life experiences.

I love the feeling of freedom that comes with traveling. It's different from being stuck geographically or financially (which are often connected). We can feel stuck when we want to be somewhere else but can't for whatever reason, and it can definitely seem as though it's out of our control.

With my love of travel and this call to the nations, I jumped at the chance to go on a mission trip with the pastor at our large church in Orlando. I even sold my precious camcorder, a fancy toy I was very proud of. However, none of the other money for that trip came together, and we needed the money from the camcorder just to live on. I began to get discouraged.

I told you about our mission trip soon after we founded our church, where a quarter of the congregation went to Trinidad and Tobago—the quarter on which God wanted to build the foundation of the church. That was a powerful event but so was another time when a friend invited me on a trip with him to a bunch of (very cold) countries. It was expensive, and we'd only recently started the church. As we prayed about it, my church staff, Gail, and I all felt like I should go, but I decided I'd only do it if God confirmed it.

Well, a woman in our church, a snowbird, sent a check with the explanation that she felt like it was to go for missions. *Okay*, I remember thinking, *I guess I'm going!* God confirmed it, and I would do it.

That trip to Newfoundland opened doors and began relationships there and elsewhere in Canada that we have still today. I had the chance to speak to the youth while my friend preached to the adults, and many people were saved, healed, and filled by the Spirit. We then went to Iceland, and frankly, it didn't seem to go as well. My friend had to head

home earlier than I did, and I preached at a mid-week meeting. The power of God hit that place, and God changed so many lives! Not only that, I've been back to Iceland over thirty times!

God isn't done with this call to minister to the nations, but first, He had to set me free of issues that were holding me captive financially. As I write this, I've been to seventy-eight countries. Travel obviously slowed down because of COVID, but right before I began writing this, I was able to go to Budapest, Hungary because a dear friend from Poland introduced me to some great pastors there and is even helping me get connected to several more eastern European countries!

When we sit in the same place day after day, whether it's a cubicle at work or even our family room, we can easily settle into the idea that this is our world. The horizons narrow, and we get stagnant. We settle. We think our whole world consists of our little circle, and the possibilities of life pass us by.

It's easy to get trapped in our day-to-day lives, going through the motions at home, work, or school. Financial trouble can close the door on vacations and seemingly limit our ability to break free. But God's desire for you is to dream big. "Only ask, and I will give you the nations as your inheritance, the whole earth as your possession" (Psalm 2:8, NLT).

He is telling you to ask! Dream big—not on your own, but with Him.

> **GOD IS TELLING YOU TO ASK! DREAM BIG—
> NOT ON YOUR OWN, BUT WITH HIM.**

I'm not opposed to the idea of a bucket list, but Gail and I decided that we preferred to have a vision board—a way to write things down and show them visually so that we can see what we want to do. Gail is not a natural traveler like me, and while she doesn't like airplanes, she likes the places they go. So I asked her where she wanted to go, and a trip to Mount Rushmore, Yellowstone, and the Grand Tetons was a much better fit for her, so we had a wonderful time planning that trip.

However you do it, I encourage you to enlarge your world. God wants to stretch your territory, to expand the four walls around your thinking, so you will dream together with Him. God is asking you, "Where would you like to go? I am the God of the universe, and I want to show you the beauty of My creation with your own eyes." It might be something as simple as a vacation, maybe even going to a local camping area. Or perhaps it's a family mission trip, not to Timbuktu but perhaps just across the border. The point is, God wants to stretch you.

And the best part? After He stretches you, you will never return to being your original shape and size.

Sometimes being stuck is as simple as being trapped in the four walls of your life where you have stopped dreaming and envisioning possibilities. It might be because of reasons you feel are outside your control—generational, financial, or even physical. There is an inertia to being stuck, an opposing force that holds you still that takes effort to break. A body at rest tends to stay at rest, but a body in motion also tends to stay in motion. God wants to break you out, so you can regain movement in your life and experience freedom!

Geographical freedom and physical movement are just representations of a couple of ways we can get unstuck and help build positive inertia. I find it can be very powerful to get up and get moving, doing anything. It doesn't have to be some large bucket-list item; it might just be a day drive or going somewhere different or scenic to eat a picnic of cheap food from the grocery store. Don't let financial lenses that say you can't afford it limit you from doing something—anything—that gets you up and moving. Make some memories with your kids, even if you don't have any money to do unique things with them. The vast majority of the time, they just want to connect with you anyway, and you can do that at a neighborhood park.

STUCK

I firmly believe that God wants to expand your picture with a bigger view, and that might simply begin with a change of scenery. I know people in Ocala, Florida, who have never been to Disney World or the beach, even though we're only about an hour and a half away. I'm not making fun of them; we were all pretty stuck for a long time during the height of the pandemic. But I think God has something more adventurous in mind for us.

Don't let the negative inertia of COVID-19 or anything else keep you bound and stuck. The small walls of the mundane want to hold you in, but God is the God who sets us free. He created the universe, and it is still expanding! He wants us to dream and have visions beyond what is right in front of us, so we can see a bigger picture in a bigger view.

Listen to the promise that God gave to Abraham:

Leave your native country, your relatives, and your father's family, and go to the land that I will show you. I will make you into a great nation. I will bless you and make you famous, and you will be a blessing to others. I will bless those who bless you and curse those who treat you with contempt. All the families on earth will be blessed through you.
—Genesis 12:1-3 (NLT)

Notice that God doesn't tell him where to stop—He just tells him to go. And consider this for a moment: Abraham was not the first one in the family God told to move. He had told Abraham's father as well, but he stopped and settled in a land that was not his destination. Abraham's brother—Lot's father—died, and Abraham's father never got over it. He became stuck there in the city where his son died, and he never progressed any further.

God wants more for you than this! Yes, you may have difficult things happen to you. We live in a fallen world, and life can be very difficult. But do not let it make you stop short of the land God has promised you. Do not camp out in your grief and stay stuck in what is safe and familiar; keep going, keep walking, and seek the next thing God has for you.

RICHARD PERINCHIEF

DO NOT CAMP OUT IN YOUR GRIEF AND STAY STUCK IN WHAT IS SAFE AND FAMILIAR; KEEP GOING, KEEP WALKING, AND SEEK THE NEXT THING GOD HAS FOR YOU.

We can do this because God has given us a message—He is with us. He gives us dreams and ambitions, places to go and things to see and do. Just like Abraham, and just like Joshua who came after him, He is telling you,

Now therefore, arise, go over this Jordan, you and all this people, to the land which I am giving to them—the children of Israel. Every place that the sole of your foot will tread upon I have given you, as I said to Moses. From the wilderness and this Lebanon as far as the great river, the River Euphrates, all the land of the Hittites, and to the Great Sea toward the going down of the sun, shall be your territory. No man shall be able to stand before you all the days of your life; as I was with Moses, so I will be with you. I will not leave you nor forsake you. Be strong and of good courage, for to this people you shall divide as an inheritance the land which I swore to their fathers to give them. —Joshua 1:2-6 (NKJV)

It's time to get up. It's time to leave behind the four walls of your thinking, not necessarily for a geographical promised land, but one in your spirit. It is time to leave behind the old mindset that has you stuck, the idea that generational tendencies or factors beyond your control can hold you back from seizing God's adventurous plan for your life and embracing it to the full! Break their authority over you; write out an agreement with God embracing every possibility that He has dreamed of for you or whatever else He tells you to do

You are bound no longer. It is time to arise and go. The best part? He is with you every step of the way!

CHAPTER 8

WHERE ARE YOU?

How did I get here? If you're stuck, you've probably asked yourself this many times. If you're an analytical person, it's easy to start blaming yourself—or others, including God—for where you are. The tendency to do this is as old as humanity, beginning in the Garden of Eden with Adam himself.

God asked Adam the ultimate inventory question: "Where are you?"

"I'm here because of the woman You gave me," he replied. And Eve? She did the same thing with the serpent. We've been passing the buck ever since.

My philosophy has always been that you can't break through until you get completely honest with yourself and God about where you really are and what season you're in. So, where are you?

I want you to take a few moments to do some soul searching. Don't think of excuses or the lies we tell ourselves to feel better, and don't just say, "It's all my fault." Instead, honestly, sit back and evaluate; ask God for clarity. Where are you right now? Are you frustrated, exhausted, and near the end of your rope? Or are you still fighting by yourself, unready to accept that God is the One who wants to engage with you intimately so that you can see your next step through His eyes?

In my ministry, I've seen people I knew needed Jesus, who were so close to accepting Him . . . but they could not get past themselves. They

were overthinking, trying to punish themselves, or thinking they had to do things to get cleaned up before God would be ready to accept them. In fact, God was willing—they were the holdouts. Many of these people have one thing in common, and I want you to look at it carefully for yourself.

Many of these people didn't want to—or felt like they couldn't—forgive themselves. They recognized their need for Jesus and understood He was the path to freedom, but for one reason or another, they were not ready to let go of what was holding them back and forgive themselves, so they could receive God's forgiveness through Jesus Christ.

> **IF YOU'RE OVERTHINKING HOW STUCK YOU ARE, YOU AREN'T GOING TO BE LOOKING AT THE SOLUTION—YOUR FOCUS IS GOING TO STAY ON THE PROBLEM.**

Part of getting unstuck is forgiving ourselves. All too often, we hold ourselves back with unnecessary baggage and guilt. If you're overthinking how stuck you are, you aren't going to be looking at the solution—your focus is going to stay on the problem. Therefore, we're going to spend this chapter not looking at the problem but at how you are to see it from God's perspective. And I'll give this away as a spoiler—God is not problem-oriented. He is ready for you to let go of whatever is holding you back, so He can walk with you into your future! However, if you don't forgive yourself, you're holding yourself back from the freedom you so desperately crave.

What is that solution? Some of you may think I'm preaching that it's this magical God solution; He's going to wave His hand and fix it all if we just get pious enough. If that's what you're thinking, I have missed the mark of trying to show you the path. We aren't looking for God to instantly fix our problems.

We are connecting with God in a relationship, so He can use where we are—right now—for His glory and our good. In the context of relationship, God can then show you the next step. Does He sometimes part the Red Sea, set us free from prison, and tell us that we'll find a place with fresh paint and new carpet? You bet He does! But never forget this—God is more interested in who you are becoming than your convenience, and if you let Him, He will use everything going on in every season of your life to help draw you closer to Him. There, close to God, is where you will find that being stuck isn't what it used to be. The hopelessness, the confusion, and all the rest change when we're in His presence, content with the season we're in even when nothing seems to be happening.

So where are you? If the answer is anywhere other than "close to God," He has some work yet to do. And that's exciting! Don't spend one more minute feeling bad about that because it's time to draw closer to Him than ever before.

If your honest answer was that you feel far from God, you might be feeling like God went away from you. If you feel that way right now, I will tell you something—it's not because He moved. When we feel far from God, it's because we've moved. The good news is that God is right there waiting for us.

A well-known proverb says, "Trust in the Lord with all your heart; do not depend on your own understanding. Seek his will in all you do, and he will show you which path to take" (Proverbs 3:5-6, NLT). Instead of "seek His will," another translation says, "acknowledge Him," but the point I want to make is that when we pursue Him, He helps us. He directs us and leads us, not just to freedom but to Him.

A lot of acknowledging God is simply turning away from where you've been focused—on your own stuff—and looking up. But

unfortunately, we're the generation who constantly looks down at our phones, creating job security for chiropractors!

God has never gone anywhere, but we may not be focused on Him, and that's when He can seem the most distant. I'm reminded that after the resurrection, Jesus appeared to two disciples walking to Emmaus. The Bible tells us that He walked with them and talked with them, but they were prevented from understanding it was Jesus until He revealed Himself when He broke bread with them. I believe that as we walk on the road of grief, pain, and brokenness that come in bitter seasons, God is right there alongside us, but we may not see Him.

Remember, He tells us, "As I was with Moses, so I will be with you. I will not leave you nor forsake you" (Joshua 1:5, NKJV). Elsewhere, we read, "And I am convinced that nothing can ever separate us from God's love. Neither death nor life, neither angels nor demons, neither our fears for today nor our worries about tomorrow—not even the powers of hell can separate us from God's love" (Romans 8:38, NLT).

His love is always there. He is always there. However, you may not always perceive Him.

I used to really wrestle with why that happens. Why does God allow us to go through seasons where we feel like He's not with us? It comes back to the blame thing I mentioned earlier. As a pastor, I've lost count of how many times someone has asked me why, if God is real, He allowed something bad to happen. If He's all-powerful, they argue, then He can't be good; if He's good, then He can't be all-powerful because evil exists in the world. You may feel a little like that when you're stuck.

The thing is, we live in a fallen world. Just because something happens doesn't make it God's will. It's not God's will for bad things to happen, but He has given the earth to the children of men. We're earth's managers, and if bad things are happening and the world is a mess, it's not because of the Owner; it's because the managers ceded the deed of planet Earth over to the enemy, the prince of this earth.

If you're stuck, it isn't God's fault. It's time to stop blaming Him and be honest enough to take a hard look at where we find ourselves and the decisions that got us there. However, while God is not responsible for you being stuck and feeling alone, He is ready and waiting for you to seek Him and acknowledge Him so that He can show you how He sees it. What may seem like "stuck" to you may be something else to Him. Let's find out how God may be viewing where you are right now.

Ecclesiastes 3:1-2 (NLT) says, "For everything there is a season, a time for every activity under heaven. A time to be born and a time to die. A time to plant and a time to harvest." It's such a good scripture, they wrote a song about it! I like to look at it like this: There's a time in our lives when things begin to emerge, like spring. Then, there is a summer, where they ripen and become full. Then there's a season for harvest, but there's also a winter when everything looks dead.

However, while wintertime may make everything appear to be dead, the truth is that some of the most important work is going on under the surface during the winter seasons. Roots are going deep, and God is at work secretly in the dark places that can appear to be a grave. But it's not a grave; it's just the winter. The spring will come. When you feel stuck, you can begin to think that nothing will ever change. That's why hope is so important. And I'm not just talking about having hope that things will change; hope placed in God Himself will never disappoint.

It's important to understand the idea of seasons because I'm convinced that sometimes our "winters" can actually be sabbaths. God created the world, and on the last day, He rested—not because He was tired but because He put cycles and seasons into His creation and modeled rest for us. On the sabbath, the Jews did not work; they rested. We need time off just like plants need winter for their roots to grow. Nearly all sports have halftimes and quarters because they know athletes need a break. Sometimes, when we're stuck, we are supposed to quit fighting it and start resting.

STUCK

Many years ago I had the privilege of getting to know a legendary man of God from New Zealand named Winkie Pratney. He was an avid competitive tennis player even into his fifties. Already several years older than I, he invited me to play some tennis at the hotel where we were hosting him. At one point, I thought I was doing pretty well and that he might be slowed by his age. Not so! He was like smoke and could just crush the ball.

As we were taking a break, he told me something interesting. He was trained as a scientist, and he said to me that the reason professional tennis players take short rest periods between sets is that when the human body rests for ninety seconds, your leg muscles can actually rejuvenate themselves. So if you'll just take a little break, you can recover in order to perform better. (By the way, the rest didn't help me at all in our match. I don't think I won more than a few points.)

If you want to be released, you must learn when it's a time for restoration.

So what is it? you might be wondering. Didn't I just say in another chapter that pushing through is a secret to getting unstuck and that we need to learn to persevere? So, are we to push through or take a break? Yes.

This is why it's vital to have a good relationship with God—to stop blaming Him and be honest with yourself about where you are. Because in one situation, He may have you push through, and the next time He may tell you to rest. If you try to handle each case the same way, you can see why it wouldn't work. You must connect with the Holy Spirit of the living God; you need to hear Him speak to you about whether you should push through or you should rest.

We all may resist the winter and fear its coming, but God does some of His best work in the dark, cold quiet of the winter. And, I'll tell you this from experience: if you resist God's attempts to give you a break, eventually, you will be forced to take one.

The Israelites were supposed to let the land rest every seven years and rotate their crops and fields so that the land itself got a break. We know scientifically that the soil needs to be restored, so wise farmers ensure their land gets the restoration it needs. But over the generations, Israel did not do this. Eventually, though, the ground got its rest—when Israel was in exile. While they were gone, much of the land lay fallow for decades, and it got its rest.

But I'm pretty sure the Israelites just felt stuck.

For many, COVID-19 felt like this—stuck at home. Yet, many discovered (or rediscovered) the value of being home with their families. While some felt trapped, others saw it as a chance to rest. And, you know what? Many aren't going to return to the hectic lifestyle they were living. Now, as our country and the world emerge from that pandemic stage, we'll be able to look back and see that it was just a season.

God is strategic; He knows how you'll need to be positioned for the next thing coming. He knows how much you need to prepare and how long winter needs to be to get the root depth you'll need for the coming season.

> **WHAT YOU'RE EXPERIENCING MAY NOT BE STUCK AT ALL; IT MAY BE A FORCED SABBATH, A TIME-OUT IN THE GAME OF LIFE THAT LETS YOU CATCH YOUR BREATH AND RESTORES YOU, SO YOU CAN RISE UP AT THE RIGHT TIME.**

It's important to know that what you're experiencing may not be stuck at all; it may be a forced sabbath, a time-out in the game of life that lets you catch your breath and restores you, so you can rise up at the right time. You may be a Type A personality with high energy and

drive, and the winter seasons feel unnatural and hard for you. But I'm telling you that the sooner you learn to take your rest when it comes, the sooner you can get on board with God and receive the restoration He wants to give you.

Stuck doesn't have to be bad. Yes, that seems bizarre to say in a book about getting unstuck, but breaks aren't punishment or because you did something wrong any more than time-outs are for basketball players. God isn't sitting you with your nose in the corner because you did something wrong; He may be helping to restore your energy for the next stage of the game.

None of this is an excuse for being lazy, but if you're a Type A, that's not your problem. Times that look unproductive are your problem, but remember, those can be some of the most productive times of all. I'm reminded of the Chinese bamboo, which doesn't break through the ground for five long years. For five years, it just sits there, apparently doing nothing. Then, it can grow nearly a hundred feet tall in just five weeks!

You can't always go by your feelings. For example, you may feel horrible because you think you're stuck, but if you're where God wants you to be, doing what He wants you to do, then despite your feelings, you are not truly stuck.

You're preparing.

You're restoring. You're quietly, perhaps even imperceptibly, growing. And then, one day, it will be time, and all the quiet preparation you and God have done in the shadows will spring up into the light!

God is never stuck. Read that again—God is never stuck. He is with you, working with you and on you for your good. He is already going before you into your future to do things on your behalf.

I already told you the story about how we narrowly missed a major overreach right before the recession of 2008, but much more recently, we knew it was time to build. I was determined not to make mistakes I had in the past, so I brought it before the congregation that we needed a new building—not that God was telling us we needed to build, but we practically needed more space. I urged everyone to pray, and I told everyone that I did not have a prophecy or word on this, but I asked them to step out with me if they were willing. As a congregation, we agreed to take the initial steps of looking at the engineering and architectural details involved, but what I didn't want to do was beat the drum for three years in an extensive fundraising campaign. On the other hand, we had equity, and I felt that we would be able to get funding.

However, banking changed during the pandemic, and I couldn't even get anyone to call me back. We wanted to talk about increasing our credit limit, but at first, we heard nothing; then, we had a few false starts. We even got so far as working with the bank's vice president, but then the underwriting didn't go through because of the way we had our advisory board set up! It was a gut punch because I thought this would be it, and we'd finally get moving.

Instead, we stayed stuck. However, I began to feel God was working, and we simply didn't see it. I decided that I would lean into God's timing, so I began to pray that I would trust God and His timing for us.

Eventually, we connected with a bank that our contractor knew, and we thought it would work. It looked positive, but they kept saying they would have something for us in just a couple of weeks. Six months later, we finally received a proposal from them . . . and it was horrible! Everything was in their favor, including that they could renegotiate interest rates every year.

I told the church that we had been given an offer to do the financing, but it stunk. After nearly three years of desiring to build, we finally had an opportunity, and it was not a good one! I asked everyone to continue to pray, even as we turned down the offer. I had no idea what we were to do next.

The next day, a flurry of phone calls resulted in an introduction to a pastor in Cleveland, Ohio, who brokered church loans as a side

business. Breakthrough! The result was he felt so strongly about our construction project that he felt he could get us a letter of intent from a highly qualified lender within twenty-one days; and we received it, not in six months but in just twenty-one days! Not only that, I desired to work on this book, and the same kind of divine connection that I made that very week ended up helping to publish this book as well!

Two significant issues that I had been praying about for years, both appeared stuck for so long, began to come together within days of each other!

As of this writing, we closed on the construction loan as promised, have gone through a tedious permitting process (and finally received them), and site work is going on. Materials have been ordered, and we should be in our new multipurpose building within ten months or so. It feels like a dream come true after years of being stuck on hold!

I remember praying, "God, I knew You would do this! I knew You would come through." I called it our "season of suddenlies," because suddenly all these things were happening as the season turned from one of silent winter growth into a vibrant spring explosion!

When you're stuck, you probably have many questions for God. Why is this happening? When will it be over? Is this my fault? How many laps around Jericho must I march before the wall comes down?

But it's important to understand that God has questions for you! As with Adam, God asks you, "Where are you?" It's an inventory question—He already knows, but He wants you to come to terms with it. If you feel stuck right now, God may be asking you, "Who told you that you were stuck?"

Remember, for Adam and Eve, the answer to that question was the serpent. Remember, our enemy is a liar. How can you tell if he's lying? His lips are moving! If you want to know the truth about your situation, there is only one source: God. Go to God for answers—and not to your own questions but His!

RICHARD PERINCHIEF

> **IF YOU WANT TO KNOW THE TRUTH ABOUT YOUR SITUATION, THERE IS ONLY ONE SOURCE: GOD. GO TO GOD FOR ANSWERS—AND NOT TO YOUR OWN QUESTIONS BUT HIS!**

In the Gospels, Jesus asked some people if they wanted to be healed. In another place, He asked two blind men who were crying out for mercy, "What do you want me to do for you?"

"'Lord,' they said, 'we want to see!' Jesus felt sorry for them and touched their eyes. Instantly, they could see! Then they followed him" (Matthew 20:33-34, NLT).

What do you want God to do for you? Of course, you probably want to be free, but I would ask you to carefully consider this question because if you are in a season of quiet winter growth, you may want to pray a prayer different than "Get me unstuck!"

You may want to pray and ask God to show you the way forward, to be the lamp to your feet and the light to your path. You may want to acknowledge Him and ask Him to direct your path and make your way straight.

It may not be time for explosive growth; it may be time for rest, restoration, and rejuvenation. Perhaps you are in a time of sabbath, and instead of fighting it, you need to embrace it, and ask God to help you get everything out of it that He wants for you.

Whatever you ask, my prayer for you is that God would help you see through His eyes and shut out the voices and questions of this world in order to listen as His still small voice asks you the most powerful questions. When He does that, the option is up to you: will you make a mad push for the exit, sick of being stuck? Or will you be willing to sit with Him, in whatever season you find yourself, and have an

honest conversation with the God of the universe about your next season and steps?

The good news is spring follows winter each and every year without fail. There is a season for everything, including the stuck of winter. And if it's winter for you right now, get ready—spring is coming!

CHAPTER 9

SUPERNATURAL, NOT SUPERHUMAN

God designed your life to be supernatural. You—yes, you—can hear the voice of God.

How do I know? Because He says so.

Getting saved in the Presbyterian church, I did not know this to be true for the first part of my life. People who "heard from God" were questionable at best, crazy at worst. I hadn't even been exposed to many people who claimed it.

However, all of that changed for me when Gail and I were filled with the Holy Spirit. We moved into a different world, and the idea of hearing from God, personally, began to enter our spiritual lives.

One of the passages that changed my life was John 10, where Jesus said, "My sheep hear My voice, and I know them, and they follow Me. And I give them eternal life, and they shall never perish; neither shall anyone snatch them out of My hand" (John 10:27-28, NKJV).

Are you saved? Then you are one of His sheep. He is your Shepherd. He calls you by name, and you can hear His voice.

You were born with the capability to hear His voice, just like I was. But until God opened my spiritual ears when Gail and I received the

Holy Spirit, I didn't know I could do so, nor had I practiced it. And, yes, hearing from God is both something you're born with and something you practice. God designed our lives to be more than just natural; He created us to also operate in the supernatural. I like to say that you don't have to be Superman, super-spiritual, or superficial; He designed you to be supernatural.

John 14:12 (NKJV) says something mind-blowing, "Most assuredly, I say to you, he who believes in Me, the works that I do he will do also; and *greater* works than these he will do because I go to My Father" (emphasis mine). How can we do greater works than Jesus? It seems almost blasphemous to say that.

There's only one way for this to happen—by the power of His Holy Spirit, the same Spirit that empowered Jesus Himself.

John the Baptist introduced repentance and water baptism, but Jesus told His disciples that He would baptize them with a gift far greater, the Holy Spirit. It's the only way we'd have the power to do the greater works He said we would do. Acts 1:8 (NKJV) promises this: "But you shall receive power when the Holy Spirit has come upon you; and you shall be witnesses to Me in Jerusalem, and in all Judea and Samaria, and to the end of the earth."

In his letter to the Philippians, Paul instructed:

Be energetic in your life of salvation, reverent and sensitive before God. That energy is God's energy, an energy deep within you, God himself willing and working at what will give him the most pleasure"
—Philippians 2:13 (MSG)

That energy is the power of the Holy Spirit. He empowers us to "do everything readily and cheerfully—no bickering, no second-guessing allowed! Go out into the world uncorrupted, a breath of fresh air in this squalid and polluted society. Provide people with a glimpse of good living and of the living God. Carry the light-giving Message into the night" (Philippians 2:14-15, MSG).

RICHARD PERINCHIEF

Your life is about giving others anointed glimpses of God, greater works than Jesus did because He only walked this earth for thirty-three years. Yet, you are here today bearing His image, His name, and His miracle-working power to carry His light-giving message into a dark world.

Without the Holy Spirit, we lack the power to do what God calls us to do. Luke 9:1-2 (GW) describes our mission:

Jesus called the twelve apostles together and gave them power and authority over every demon and power and authority to cure diseases. He sent them to spread the message about God's kingdom and to cure the sick.

What has Jesus given us power and authority over? Some demons? To do some healings? Half? Maybe 99 percent of demons are under the authority of His name? No—the Holy Spirit within us gives us power and authority over every demon and to cure the sick. If we truly mean to carry out a greater mission than that of Jesus Himself, we need the Spirit that empowered Jesus's earthly ministry!

And we cannot do so with the freedom and perspective that He wishes for us if we're stuck. So I want to tell you this plainly: The Holy Spirit is the One who sets us free.

We read, "But the Holy One has anointed you and you all know the truth" (1 John 2:20, TPT). I love how it says you will know all the truth because of the famous Scripture that we will know the truth, and the truth will set us free. Another version puts it like this: "For if you embrace the truth, it will release true freedom into your lives" (John 8:32, TPT).

Before I embraced the Truth as a living Person, I was not set free. So my prayer for all of us is that God will supernaturally open the eyes of our hearts so that we can activate the truth He had put within our hearts when we accepted Jesus—and that this Truth will set us free every time we are stuck.

UNSTUCK

If you're a follower of Christ Jesus, you're not trying to be perfect. You're not trying to be this holy person with a halo. You're just trying to be the best version of yourself that you can be, with Jesus's help and power within you to accomplish God's plan for you on this planet.

In practical terms, this doesn't mean you'll never get stuck, never be in a bad mood, or never have anything bad happen to you. It does mean, however, that when you get stuck, you know Whom to go to. You have power thanks to Him, and you're not subject to the god of this world. Instead, you are a new creation. The old has passed away, and you've been made new because Christ is within you.

Remember, every believer has already received the call to ministry. It may not be as a pastor, evangelist, or missionary, so don't let that cause you to shut down or intimidate you into assuming you're supposed to be something you're not. The ministry God has called you to is not dependent on you; it's dependent on Him. It doesn't mean you have to do what I do. Even if you've never felt goosebumps or a lightning bolt during prayer, you have a call of God—and it is unique to you.

As a kid, I couldn't imagine something more boring than being a pastor. As I mentioned before, I ran from the infant call in my heart, but I didn't understand God's ultimate picture for me or what it would entail. Now I can't imagine not being a pastor! God is not up in heaven cooking up random calls for us; He is a good, good Father who understands intimately how He made us and what will bring our hearts fulfillment and bring Him glory.

If you are afraid of the call of God on your life, it is a spirit of fear and intimidation. It's a lie! It's fake news, and part of getting unstuck is breaking its hold over your life, so the truth can free you. God has not given you this spirit of fear; instead, He gives you a Spirit of power, love, and a sound mind (see 2 Timothy 1:7).

God is the One who gives you the power and authority, through the Holy Spirit living in you, to live an anointed everyday life. He is the

One who gave you your talents and abilities and desires, even if they are hidden or pushed down.

Your ministry is likely not from a pulpit but instead may be in an SUV full of kids, an office, or a dugout coaching a Little League team. God will align your heart with His if you submit your will to His.

We have Jesus as a model in this. In the Garden of Gethsemane before His crucifixion, Jesus prayed, "Father, if it is Your will, take this cup away from Me; nevertheless not My will, but Yours, be done" (Luke 22:42, NKJV). Jesus understood the joy that was set before Him—our salvation. It's why He was here on earth.

God is not calling you to do something that is against the way He made you; He's calling you to do His will in sync with the way He made you from when you were in your mother's womb. And when we struggle to accept His will, we pray along with Jesus, "Not my will but yours."

We need to redefine what ministry actually is. You see, nearly all the dictionaries have the wrong definition of calling and ministry. They usually make it sound so religiously formal and traditional; like ministry is all about rituals and theological regulations—which it is not. In the church, people talk about the five-fold ministry of apostles, prophets, evangelists, pastors, and teachers, but they forget that those are not all the ministry there is. That is just the hand of the body of Christ; there's the whole rest of the body left. Every one of us is called because all of us are necessary.

Ephesians 4:11 describes the five-fold ministry, but 4:12 (TPT) describes the true purpose for people in these positions of full-time ministry:

Their calling is to nurture and prepare all the holy believers to do their own works of ministry, and as they do this they will enlarge and build up the body of Christ.

Why do we need pastors like me and all the rest? To equip you to do your own works of ministry!

Too many try to make it out as though only these full-time ministers can have a call of God and do the more wondrous works Jesus promised.

They're expecting Clergy Man, the Christian superhero, who prays with power, heals the sick, or prophesies God's words of encouragement. People think that Clergy Man will fly in, wearing his ornate robe, and do the "work of God" because only he is qualified.

It's a lie! You, a holy believer, are called to do your own works of ministry that help the body of Christ and carry Jesus's message of salvation to those who don't know Him yet.

The idea that those who do God's will are clergy and the rest are laypeople is just ridiculous. What even is a layman? Someone who lays around? Lay around at home, lay around at work, lay around at church—doing nothing. That is not what Jesus said you would do. Clergy aren't "on high" while laypeople are down in the dirt. Yes, those in full-time ministry have a piece of paper, but let me share a secret with you: You don't need a piece of paper to do works of ministry. All you need is the Holy Spirit empowering you!

Those of us in full-time ministry are to provide every believer with the tools and weapons to accomplish your ministry and to build up the body of Christ. It's like a trainer or a coach. If you watch football on TV, I challenge you to find the strength and conditioning coach on the sideline. You won't because it's not about the coaches; it's about the players. And that's you—you are the players on the field, and I'm just a minor coach on staff.

I'm telling you all of this because your misconceptions, fears, and intimidations can keep you stuck, locked in a lie that prevents you from stepping into God's works He has prepared for you from the foundations of the earth. God wants His truth to set you free and His Holy Spirit to empower you to greater works because a handful of us ministering from pulpits cannot possibly do the full extent of God's mission for His body on the earth.

Instead, God wants you to use all your God-given talents, abilities, and resources to serve others and to fulfill the divine assignment and purpose for which you were born. That is my definition of ministry, and when you step out in it, the very gates of hell itself cannot hold you back from accomplishing God's purpose for you on this earth!

You may be anointed to excel at business or parenting or teaching or athletics—anything can be part of God's call on your life, and it is my passion to see you set free to accomplish whatever God has set before you. Wherever you are, you can be supernatural in that setting, from working in a factory to crunching numbers in an office to wiping snotty noses at home.

> **WHEREVER YOU ARE, YOU CAN BE SUPERNATURAL IN THAT SETTING, FROM WORKING IN A FACTORY TO CRUNCHING NUMBERS IN AN OFFICE TO WIPING SNOTTY NOSES AT HOME.**

Don't let the enemy push you down and try to keep you locked up when God wants to do something extraordinary in your life!

The people of the world are hungry for a supernatural source of power. They're not looking for new religion right now; they're looking for something spiritual, something supernatural. They're hungry for more.

Why do you think we see so many supernatural-themed shows and movies? Look at all the superhero movies that have come out over the last decade or so. People are hungry for power that can change things and save them. They want to know power is available and real, and they want to think that it can intersect our daily lives.

As people look for power, I want them to see Christians and take note. People notice lives that flat-out work. In a world of craziness and dysfunction, people are hungry to encounter those who have a power

source that enables them to function anyway. So, let's not show them Clergy Man or the Avengers. Instead, let's show them your super(natural) powers as a Spirit-filled believer in action!

If we want to blow their minds, we can show them God's peace in our lives when everything around us is going up in flames. Show them joy when circumstances say we should be depressed. Show them love when the natural response is bitterness and anger. I don't mean we fake it; I mean that we tap into the supernatural power of God to respond to our life situations with the resources He makes available through the Holy Spirit within us.

There are many counterfeits. When I worked in insurance, I collected money from a family of "seers." They claimed they could see into the future, and people would pay them money to tell them their fortunes. The problem was, they were always broke when I came to get their insurance payments! Why would you pay someone who is broke to tell you the future? It would be like going to marriage counseling with Elizabeth Taylor, an old-time movie star who married eight times. It didn't work, and people could tell.

Some people believe in luck. I watch college football as every player needs to do whatever little gesture they do for luck, like tapping the door or patting the gator. Of course, we all know that doesn't work; just look at their win record! Others won't even leave the house until they've checked their horoscope, but I've always wondered why you'd direct your life according to something that sounds like "horror"! Recently someone told me they were a Capricorn and asked what I was; I wanted to shoot back, "I'm a blood-bought child of God!"

While some look to the stars or for signs or omens, the problem is that according to Jesus, the signs will follow us! Jesus promised, "And these signs will follow those who believe: In My name they will cast out demons; they will speak with new tongues" (Mark 16:17, NKJV).

There's nothing like the real thing, and no substitute or counterfeit can replace the power of God. Isaiah told us:

RICHARD PERINCHIEF

When people tell you, "Try out the fortunetellers. Consult the spiritualists. Why not tap into the spirit-world, get in touch with the dead?" Tell them, "No, we're going to study the Scriptures." —Isaiah 8:19-20 (MSG)

The answer isn't mysticism, spirituality, superstition, or magic—it's the supernatural power of God. None of those fakes is the answer to your stuck. If you've tried them, it's time to repent and turn to Him alone.

When I was around thirteen, I asked my loving parents for a Ouija board, thinking it was just a game from Milton Bradley. The problem is, you need at least two people to "play," and no one would play with me! Well, a few days after my birthday was Easter, and my crazy aunt from New Jersey, who was a discerning intercessor and saw God's call on my life long before I did, came into town. She asked me what I got for my birthday, and I showed her the Ouija board and asked her to play with me.

She said, "No, no, I'll do something better. I'll give you $30 for it—if you promise you'll never touch another one in your life." (At the time, it probably cost less than $8.) I told her for $30.00, she could have my sister too! Thirty dollars sounded like a fortune to me, and I never did touch one again in my life. I have no idea what doors the Lord kept closed because she made that deal with me.

Plenty of people think this and other things are just harmless fun and games, but they open the door of your life to demonic power. I was an innocent thirteen-year-old who didn't know any better. You may have been innocent too if you've tried these things. However, you can still "innocently" open the door to the wrong things in your life—and experience the consequences of letting darkness have access to you.

Recent surveys show that over one-half of young people raised in the church think there are many ways to heaven. But the Bible tells us that there is no "salvation in any other, for there is no other name under heaven given among men by which we must be saved" (Acts 4:12, NKJV). Salvation comes only through Him. That name is Jesus, who was elevated to the place of highest honor and to Whom God gave the

name that is higher than any other—that at the name of Jesus, every knee should bow (see Philippians 2:9-10).

People are looking for power. They're looking for strength to handle this difficult life. They're looking for resources that will see them through trying times. They want a sense of identity, they want favor, and they want to see miracles—but many are looking for these things in all the wrong places.

Your call isn't to be in the dark with nothing, like people who turn to these things. Your purpose is to show the Light of the World to a dark and hurting land where there is no hope. The hope isn't you; you're just a bearer of it, a dispenser. As you walk out a supernatural life right in front of them, they will see that light. It will be unmistakable because you'll have peace in the chaos, joy in the hard times, and hope in the middle of darkness. The everyday walk of a person with the supernatural power of the Holy Spirit within them will shine brightly for all to see, and they'll be drawn to you and hungry for that something different that makes you stand out as one who has spent time with Jesus.

YES, PEOPLE ARE HUNGRY—AND THAT FOR WHICH THEY HUNGER IS FOUND ONLY IN JESUS!

Yes, people are hungry—and that for which they hunger is found only in Jesus! And if you've been looking for these things anywhere other than Christ, you are going to feel stuck. If you've been looking through the means of powerless religion and empty ceremony without the power of the Holy Spirit, you're going to be left frustrated and wanting. Salvation comes only through Jesus, but His gift to us was His Holy Spirit, the One who would empower us to carry out the purpose for which we are on this planet.

RICHARD PERINCHIEF

Whatever we look to for power we end up worshiping. Do you think that other means of connecting with the supernatural will set you free? You're in for a surprise because those very things end up tying people down in bondage. In whatever form it takes and however innocently we may start, idolatry is still destructive. It's why God gave us the command that we should have no other gods before Him—it will hurt us! God isn't trying to be egotistical. He's trying to protect us!

The moment we begin to look for power from the wrong source, we open the door, and the chains that come from that illicit connection will bind us and hold us back when God's will for us is to be free and free indeed!

The good news is we can repent today. Repenting means turning away, turning your back on what you were doing that isn't God's best for you and turn to Him and Him alone. It's turning away from the shady things of the spiritual and turning to the supernatural for which God designed you. He built you to be empowered by His Spirit, and your life is a demonstration to those around you of His goodness and glory on this earth.

If you've dabbled, I urge you to go no further until you've cried out to God right where you are. Then, ask Him to wash you and make you clean, to restore your innocence to before you tried things other than Him. He is faithful and will forgive, cleansing you of all unrighteousness.

The supernatural can be controversial, even within the body of Christ. Many denominations are afraid of what it represents. Yet, God used Paul to tell us His thoughts: "Now about the spiritual gifts [the special endowments given by the Holy Spirit], brothers and sisters, I do not want you to be uninformed" (1 Corinthians 12:1, AMP). Other versions say "ignorant" instead of uninformed, but the clear message of this passage is that while there are many types of gifts, God has intended them for all believers. Paul went on to say, "But to each one is given the manifestation of the Spirit [the spiritual illumination and the enabling of the Holy Spirit] for the common good" (1 Corinthians 12:7, AMP).

STUCK

When I talk to you about hearing from God, is there a tiny part of you that hears Scripture and reads my words that it's for everyone—and yet you add *except me* in your mind? Is there a part of you that still believes you can't do it?

I did too. In fact, I used to be the one who made fun of Christians! I thought it was all ridiculous, yet God proved His sense of humor. When I was young, a revival broke out near where I lived, and even kids from my Presbyterian church were going and getting saved by the power of God. I laughed at them, making fun of the "holy rollers" and "Jesus freaks," as I called them. Yet at nineteen years of age, I became one of them!

When I went to my ten-year high school reunion, someone had found out that I was a youth pastor, so they asked me to open the dinner with a prayer. Well, when I stood up to pray, laughter rippled through the audience. Afterward, a woman I knew got up and said, "I'm so sorry. I caused that commotion. I didn't know you were a pastor!" She smiled and asked, "Do you remember when you used to tease me on the bus and called me a holy roller?"

I nodded, embarrassed, and said, "Yes, I remember."

"Well, every time you did, I prayed for you. I didn't know you'd become a Christian! When I saw you getting up to pray, I just began to laugh uncontrollably! When they told me where you were a youth pastor, I fell off my chair laughing because I realized God has a sense of humor!"

I never expected to hear from God, certainly not when I was making fun of that girl on the bus, and she was praying for me. Yet God had something greater in mind for me, and He has something greater for you, as well! So stop limiting God and what He can do in your life, and start opening your spirit to the idea He is eager to speak with you. He created you to receive from Him, to commune with Him as Adam and Eve did in the Garden of Eden. Sin severed that connection, but Jesus did more than restore it—God put Himself within us.

You have the same Holy Spirit within you, and He is ready to help you receive from God. He is ready to whisper gently right into your heart, and your part is not to try harder and willpower your way into hearing from God.

It's to wait on God. To listen. To get quiet and set aside the time to still and quiet your soul within you so that the many noises of this world are no longer your focus. Then, when you are still and quiet before God, you can hear His gentle whisper.

If you were next to your spouse in a loud crowd, you would bend close to hear them. This is "inclining your ear." The supernatural is not always spectacular. In fact, it begins with this very ordinary thing, tuning in to the voice of God. Like God, I desire for you to experience everything that He has for you, but it doesn't start with healing services or being in full-time ministry. It begins with learning to tune in to the voice of God.

He will not compete with all the noise of the world. He is jealous of your attention, and He desires to speak with you. Greater works than those Jesus did can come, but until you're intimately connected with the heart of God, do you really want to get out there and try them? First, learn the heart of your Father—not just by learning about Him, but by conversing with Him. Stop praying a monologue and start having a dialogue with your heavenly Father.

We're going to spend the next few chapters learning more about how we connect with the Holy Spirit, who is the ongoing source of our sustained freedom. But before we do, you've got to clear the slate of all that came before. Power from any other source will hook you and hold you back. Power from God's source will set you free!

Worship generates identity because you become like whatever you worship. I don't know about you, but I want to become like the One who is peace, light, and joy. That's what I want to be like! I want to become like the One who is ultimate freedom! If that is you, join me in forsaking all others to pursue the Holy Spirit of the living God. Let's do it together—I'll show you how in the coming chapters.

CHAPTER 10

TUNE IN

About a million years ago, radios had these things called dials. A dial was a knob, not a screen or even a button; you had to turn by hand to tune in a radio station. I remember looking for a particular radio station and having it be close, but not quite right. There would be static, or the music would not be clear. You could maybe make it out if you knew the song. However, by turning the dial one way or another, you could "tune in" to the station and bring clarity to the music or words. Once you had the station dialed in, you could hear your song.

In the previous chapter, I mentioned that people have been created with the ability to hear from God but that it is also a skill that can be developed. Being born with that capacity is like having the radio—you can receive what God is sending out.

However, if you're constantly tuned in to the news, into your own interests, or into social media, for instance, and you never stop to take the time to tune in to God, you're going to miss much of what He is sending out. It will be full of static and hard to hear—if you discern it as Him at all. But if you'll take the time to tune in to God, suddenly, what He is saying becomes clearer.

One of the best stories from the Bible about hearing from God comes from the life of Elijah. After his amazing experience with God atop Mount Carmel, where Elijah faced off with all the prophets of the false god Baal and saw fire fall from heaven, he was so frightened by the queen who had threatened his life that he ran off into the wilderness. However, God met the wayward prophet even here as he ran and set up an experience that tells us a lot about God's voice.

God told Elijah,

"Go out, and stand on the mountain before the Lord." And behold, the Lord passed by, and a great and strong wind tore into the mountains and broke the rocks in pieces before the Lord, but the Lord was not in the wind; and after the wind an earthquake, but the Lord was not in the earthquake; and after the earthquake a fire, but the Lord was not in the fire; and after the fire **a still small voice.** *—1 Kings 19:11-12 (NKJV, emphasis mine)*

If we're looking for God to be big and brash like a firestorm or an earthquake, we're going to wait a long time. That's not God's MO. Instead, we hear God in what other translations call "a gentle whisper"—a still, small voice.

Now, consider this: how do you hear a whisper in a loud environment? You must listen carefully. You have to tune in; otherwise, a whisper will be easy to miss.

And, let me tell you, our world is full of loud noises. The TV offers many of them, from political commentary to sports broadcasting to reality shows and beyond. Then we've got these little mobile distraction devices right in our hands all the time that can show us virtually anything we want, any time we want. Got an empty moment? Fill it with digital noise in the palm of your hand!

But if you're constantly filling yourself with the voices of this world, they're going to be so loud that you will easily miss the still, small voice of God.

RICHARD PERINCHIEF

> **IF YOU'RE CONSTANTLY FILLING YOURSELF WITH THE VOICES OF THIS WORLD, THEY'RE GOING TO BE SO LOUD THAT YOU WILL EASILY MISS THE STILL, SMALL VOICE OF GOD.**

I think we can make hearing from God harder than it needs to be, acting as though only Clergy Man or Super Christian can hear God. However, we can also discount the fact that it does take the intentionality to tune in and listen if you want to hear the voice of God routinely.

It was a simpler, more innocent time when I was a kid. Not only did we have radios with dials, but we also had different expectations for kids. Instead of fearing for our safety all the time, our parents gave us some general rules to follow—and sent us out to play. In the street! The ground rule for most kids in the summer was, "Be home when the streetlights come on." I was free to roam the neighborhood with my friends, playing and getting into whatever situations we could, but when the lights came on, it was time to go home. And when I got home, because they'd established the rules, my parents would not say, "We wanted you home an hour ago." Why? Because they'd set the principles and then we honored them. If they wanted me to do something different, they told me.

This is a lot like the simplicity of God's connection to us. God does not change His character. He's not out there changing His mind on things. He can communicate, and He does. He has given us His principles, and we live by them. So, if He wants us to do something specific, He can and will communicate this—but we need to listen.

If my parents told me to be home by a specific time, but I wasn't listening, that was on me. The rest of the time, I operated comfortably with the knowledge that unless they said something different, I knew

their will (for me to be home when the lights came on). So let me ask you this: how are your listening skills? The burden of proof is on our heavenly Father if He wants to change something, but if you want to receive what He has to say, you do need to be listening for His whispers.

It's vital that you understand this, as well: He's not intentionally being cryptic or hard to find. He is a good, good Father, and He wants to communicate with you. How are you responding to that?

Many people I meet who struggle with the idea of hearing from God have built up reasons in their minds why they can't. Sure, other people, like preachers and such, may be able to, but maybe they think they've done too many bad things for God to speak to them. They're too busy and can't spend the hours in prayer they assume are necessary. Or perhaps they had something terrible and painful happen to them. Some believe that only people called to ministry can hear from God. That is why I spent the previous chapter trying to establish how we all are called to ministry and that as His sheep, we can all hear His voice. Not only that, we have a promise that we will be able to know His voice.

Excuses and lies about connecting with God can keep you stuck when God has made you, as His child, able to communicate with Him. You bear His image and His Spirit, and as His blood-bought child, you can learn to hear God's voice. Now, it's time to tune in and listen.

Many people ask me, "How do we do that, tune in and listen?" Let me tell you how I learned.

When Gail and I were first Spirit-filled, we commuted back and forth to that big church in Orlando for nearly a year before we decided to move there. However, we were really short on money. We needed to know God's plan for us because while we felt like we should move, we weren't sure how we'd pay for it.

I decided to seek God. I'd never really done it before, but I ended up asking my in-laws if I could borrow their mobile home for a few hours to get away and pray. I'd been Spirit-filled less than a year, but we'd been receiving good teaching, so I believed that I could hear from God. I just hadn't ever tried it before.

I went to the mobile home with my Bible and a notebook. I don't know why, but I ended up getting on the floor and writing my questions for God. One of the first things I wrote was asking God about our move to Orlando and the problem that we could not find a place. Gail was upset because we'd be leaving our home and starting over. I wanted something from God that I could tell her, especially whether we were to move now or later—or not at all.

I wrote questions to God for two or three hours, and I was beginning to get tired and bored because I was not getting anything. Then, suddenly, I had this still, small voice rise up in me! So I began to write as the Lord whispered to my heart.

It was time to move. And I felt like He said to tell Gail not to worry; our new place wouldn't be a fleabag mess. I felt God was telling me it would have new carpet and new paint. He gave me a few other things as well, but these answers to our precise questions were what I was after. When I told Gail these things, she was entirely on board, ready to move now.

That following Sunday, after church, we went with a couple of friends to look at places to rent. We poured over the newspaper and drove out to a few locations, but they weren't it. We returned very frustrated, but there at church, the security guard asked if we'd seen a particular listing. I'm not sure how we missed it. It was $420 a month and near the church.

Oh, and it had new carpet and new paint!

We went over to see it, and the friendly young owner met us. He'd just bought a house and needed to rent it out. The only downside was that it was just a two-bedroom, so our son and daughter would have to share a room. However, when we saw it, the new carpet and paint looked really good!

We explained why we were moving to Orlando, and while the guy wasn't a Christian, he liked us. "I usually require one month down and

another month as a security deposit. That would be $840. But what were you thinking of as a deposit?"

I told him, "Oh, you don't want to ask me. I was thinking zero!"

He thought for a moment. "You guys seem like nice people. I'm going to go ahead and let you move in for just one month's rent."

Now, we needed $420 by Thursday! So we went home praying because while this place had the new carpet and new paint God had told me about, we didn't have the deposit. But God wasn't done yet.

We went to my in-laws' house the day before the money was due. My wife's grandfather was living with her parents at this point, and he asked us to come back and talk to him.

"Do you believe I hear from the Man upstairs?" he said. Now, he believed in God, but he didn't have a real relationship with Jesus as far as I knew. (In fact, I had the privilege of leading him to the Lord a year or so later.)

We looked at each other. "Yes, we do," we replied.

He pulled out five one-hundred-dollar bills. We have no idea where he got them; Gail's parents had been managing his money for years! "God spoke to me and told me you need this," he told us.

It was everything we needed! The. Day. Before! Not only did God provide the rent money to move in, but the leftover was also enough to turn on our utilities.

God was beginning to teach me to hear Him, and I was blown away that He could be so specific—if I'd listen. But I had to tune in.

The easiest thing in the world is hear from God, and simultaneously, the hardest thing to do is hear from God. You were born to do it; you're His kid. But He's not going to shout down all the other noises that want to fill your life, so as you're learning to get unstuck, the best thing I can tell you is that you must learn to tune in and hear God's still, small voice.

God will not compete with our noise, and there are record amounts of noise in our world right now. We must listen!

While that was the first time I really felt like God spoke to me this way, it is certainly not the last. Perhaps the biggest was after we had begun our own church.

When we first started our own church years later, our worship stank. I don't want to be mean; we were doing our best. We were using CDs and even tapes and whatever we could. If someone could play an instrument, we had them play and lived with it.

Eventually, I did the same thing I'd done when we found our condo so we could move to Orlando—I got a notebook and ended up on the floor, asking God what to do about the music. This time, it was a day or so later before God spoke to my heart. I wrote down, "I'm sending you a psalmist. Wait for him." I was so excited—God had answered! Praise God!

Now... what was a "psalmist"? I didn't know.

As I prayed about what a psalmist was, God showed me that it was someone who could take the messages from God in the house (church) and turn them into music and worship. This was a powerful gift, and I became excited that God would prepare such a man for our church.

Now I was actively looking for our psalmist. I eventually went to a tiny church in a little town where a friend was preaching. This young man got up and started leading praise and worship. He was so talented! My friend with me leaned over and asked, "Who's that guy?"

"I don't know," I replied, "but I think he's my psalmist!"

However, I wasn't going to take someone from another church, so I wasn't sure how that would work. Yet I soon learned that he wasn't the worship leader there; he was there as a guest and had never led worship before! When my friend ended the meeting, he called up anyone who felt they were called to the ministry, and this young man, Lindsey, came to the front. My friend asked me to come and pray for people, and Lindsey ended up being the person I prayed with.

I could see God all over him! I invited him to come lead worship as a guest sometime, and a few weeks later, he did. The rest is

history—nearly thirty years together, with Lindsey becoming a son to us. If we have a family meeting, Lindsey is there. He hasn't changed his name to Perinchief, but he is one with us in spirit. Lindsey was raised by a hard-working single mom and has four older sisters. With them being so far away in Iowa, we more or less adopted him. We thought that we'd be lucky to have him at our church for just a few years because he's so insanely talented, but he has been with us all this time, and we enjoy every day of it. I am so glad that God told me to wait for a psalmist because Lindsey is all that and more! He is exactly the person God intended to meet that need.

It is easier to know God and hear His voice than you think it is, but it is also harder than your flesh wants it to be because you must lean into that and incline your ear to the Lord. I want to say that it gets easier the more you do it, and in certain ways, it does. However, that war with your flesh, which wants to tune into the loudest voice and be distracted, never ends.

I know I can't even claim ADD as an excuse; I'm more like ADOS—attention deficit, Oh! Shiny! It can be hard to push back on all the things that want our attention to be quiet enough to hear God's gentle whisper.

Not only that, listening to God is often like walking a tightrope for me. When you're there before God in prayer because you need an answer or else it will be bad for you, it's tough. But it's also exciting! You learn that even though the timing may not be what you want it to be, God is never ever late. Neither is He early. His timing is always perfect. I have seen Him come through for me time after time, and each time He does so, it builds my faith.

Being still before God and waiting on Him with my questions and notebook has become a principle for me. I get still and quiet before Him every Saturday, where I turn off absolutely everything else for a while, so I can simply listen. I get out my pen and notebook, and for an hour—sometimes just half an hour—I write my questions, and I listen for His still, small voice in my spirit.

CHAPTER 11

DISCERNING HIS VOICE

To your spirit, hearing from God is the easiest thing in the world. You were born to do it, like a baby duck imprinting on its mother. To your flesh, it's the hardest thing in the world because it requires putting your flesh down in order to tune in with your spirit. However, if you want to get unstuck—and stay unstuck—your connection to God is how to get free and stay free longer. And, when a period of stuck comes again (and it will), communicating with God is at the center of finding freedom again.

We now know how important it is to tune in to the voice of God. Remember, God won't compete for your attention. If you want to hear His still, small voice, you've got to silence all those other voices. And there are a lot of them!

The world has many voices—loud ones! The media has a voice, and they're not afraid to broadcast their message on the news 24/7. Your hobbies and interests have voices; for me, a big one is the voice of sports. Even friends and family have voices. Now, these are not necessarily bad, but neither are they the voice of the Lord.

Some voices are definitely not godly. There's the voice of your fears and insecurities. There's the voice of guilt and condemnation, bringing up the things you've done or failed to do. But, unfortunately, our enemy

also has a voice, bringing up these things and other lies and weaponizing them against you.

If you want to communicate with God well enough to get unstuck, it's vital to learn to discern God's voice.

People sometimes ask me what God's voice sounds like. First of all, remember, it's not typically an audible voice. God spoke to Elijah in a still, small voice, and I have found that most of the time, God prefers to whisper to our hearts. Jesus promises that His sheep (us) will know His voice, and the voice of a stranger they will not follow. But here's the critical part—when we hear His voice and know it, then we can activate it.

To me, there is a difference between tuning in to God and becoming familiar enough to recognize and respond to His voice. After all, you can't respond to something you don't recognize. For example, imagine you're trying to discern the voice of a new boss you've never met in a crowded meeting room. How would you know who he is? By tone? Volume? Bossiness? Now, instead, picture being in a room full of family members you know and love well. Could you pick out your father's voice in a crowd? Your mother's? Of course you could because you know them intimately.

This is what your Father God wants for you. He wants you to spend enough time in His presence to know Him, so when all the voices of this world are competing for your attention, you'll be able to pick His out from the crowd. As I mentioned in the previous chapter, part of this is about tuning in. I would argue that you can't get to know His voice unless you're quiet enough to hear a whisper. When I need to hear from God, I still get quiet and alone with my notebook, often on the floor again, and I just listen with my spiritual ears. By shutting off all those outside voices of the world, I can listen attentively enough to hear that gentle whisper.

However, you won't always have the luxury of getting alone and quiet when you need to hear God. What about when you're in a crisis and need to act immediately? Wouldn't it be nice to be able to hear from God when you need to act right now? Of course it would! That's why it's vital to get to know what His voice is like so that even in the crowded rooms of life, you can still discern His voice from all the others.

How do we do that? First, we get to know Him.

So what does God's voice sound like? I can tell you this without a doubt: He sounds like His Word. In fact, one of the first and most vital ways to learn to discern the voice of the Lord is by reading the Bible. It's God's letter to you, and He will never, ever go against His Word. God will never speak something to you that contradicts the Bible, so any voice that seems to go against the truth of the Word is obviously not God. He will not contradict Himself, so when you know the Word and its context, you're ensuring that you know His voice well enough to tell a counterfeit.

You see, the enemy knows the Word, too. When tempting Jesus in the wilderness, Satan showed that he knew the Scriptures when he quoted them out of context. Big mistake! He was debating the Word of God with the very Word made flesh, Jesus!

The devil follows what I call pretzel logic—he can quote a scripture, but he'll twist it every time. Any truth he may seem to say is always contorted by subtle lies that seem fine at first appearance, but he is a master of lies and deception and is called the father of lies. He may know the Word, but he'll use it out of context or in the wrong spirit.

The enemy will try to use the Bible to condemn, which is never God's heart, or be overly permissive—sometimes at the exact same moment! He'll try to tell you you're free to do whatever you want, and then he'll bash you over the head with guilt after you do it. He sets up traps, and he is clever enough to use a lot of truth to make them seem very appealing.

When God speaks, He will always stay consistent with the details and spirit of His Word. So when you begin to know the Bible, you begin to know God. It's so important that we are not simply reading about Him but using His Word as a way of connecting with Him.

STUCK

Think about it like this—if I gave you my social media details and you hopped online to check me out, you could learn about me. You could see my photos, you could see specific information about my life, and you may even be able to pay enough attention to discern some of my likes and dislikes. If you follow me for a while, you may see what restaurants I like or sports teams I follow. You may learn a great deal about me.

> **[THE HOLY SPIRIT] TAKES THE WRITTEN WORD OF GOD AND TURNS IT FROM WORDS ON A PAGE TALKING ABOUT GOD INTO A SPIRIT-BREATHED, LIFE-GIVING WAY OF CONNECTING WITH GOD INTIMATELY AND PERSONALLY.**

But do you really know me by reading about me? No! And this is why the Holy Spirit is so important. He takes the written Word of God and turns it from words on a page talking about God into a Spirit-breathed, life-giving way of connecting with God intimately and personally. God speaks to us through His Word, making these things written so long ago personal to you and your situation.

The Holy Spirit speaks to us with love and intimacy. He conveys the tenor of God's Word that goes beyond what the literal words say, so you can hear the tone of God's voice as He was showing people how to write it down.

Have you ever gotten a text or email that you thought was saying one thing yet actually meant something else—even though the words didn't change? I once heard a story of a young pastor who went to work for a very large church. He communicated with his boss, the lead pastor, mostly in emails. At first, a few of the emails discouraged him. Later, the lead pastor told him something that helped: "Imagine that I'm smiling when you read my emails." When the young pastor read the older man's emails with this in mind, it transformed his understanding of how the lead pastor communicated.

The tenor and tone of God's Word are important, and the Holy Spirit reveals that to your spirit. He is the One who helps you read the Word in the context of God's love and forgiveness.

I find that when people describe how God talks to them, it reveals a lot about their view of God. For example, I've heard it said, "If you want to know your future, tell me what your view of God is." A. W. Tozer said, "What comes into our minds when we think about God is the most important thing about us."[3]

Some people call Him the "Man upstairs." What comes to mind when you think of an old man upstairs? As we said earlier, he's probably upset with you for making too much noise. He'd probably yell at you to get off his grass. To many, God is a judge, a grumpy God just waiting to smack them for messing up again.

I've heard people say things such as, "The Lord spoke to me and said, 'Hey, dummy, what are you doing?'" The way they hear God reveals condemnation, mockery, or other negatives that simply aren't a part of the heart of our Father. It tells me the enemy may be twisting something, or their hurts and insecurities may influence how they hear the Lord.

Not everyone has a good relationship with their earthly father, and this can impact how people hear God. But it's important to know that God loves you with an everlasting love. He loves as no earthly father ever could, perfectly and without any of the negatives that come with our fallible earthly parents. God will never run you down, demean you, mock you, manipulate you, or anything of that nature. He is a good, good Father.

Jesus put it like this:

You fathers—if your children ask for a fish, do you give them a snake instead? Or if they ask for an egg, do you give them a scorpion? Of course

---

[3] A. W. Tozer, *The Knowledge of the Holy: The Attributes of God, Their Meaning in the Christian Life* (New Delhi, India: General Press, 2019).

STUCK

not! So if you sinful people know how to give good gifts to your children, how much more will your heavenly Father give the Holy Spirit to those who ask him. —Luke 11:11-13 (NLT)

God's heart toward you is always good. In fact, get ready for something that will blow your mind. God feels the same way about you that He feels about Jesus, His beloved Son in whom He is well pleased. He put Jesus in you, but He also put you in Jesus. So as you learn to discern the voice of God, use that as part of your criteria—if God wouldn't say it to Jesus, He wouldn't say it to you. You're His child, as surely as Jesus was His firstborn Son.

God's words to you are always redemptive. So, yes, He may sometimes correct, as he did with Gail that night when He walked her through the things He'd been dealing with in her life when we were filled with the Spirit. But He wasn't showing her those things to be punitive; He was showing her His redemptive purpose in her life. It was—and always is—for her and for our good.

You can never receive from God what you do not know Him to be for you. If you honestly tell me about your view of God, I can tell you how it will influence your ability to truly hear from Him. If you think of Him as a punisher, waiting up in heaven to nail you for messing up, you're going to have a judgmental view of God that will color your ability to hear from Him (and give your enemy fuel for twisting the Word to fit that view). I believed He was Savior and Lord, but I didn't know Him as the Baptizer in the Spirit until I started to see that in the Bible. Thank goodness for the Holy Spirit leading me to know Him deeper.

Sometimes when we're stuck, it's because our perception of God is limited. Jesus went to His hometown, but because of the people's unbelief He could not do many mighty miracles there. They didn't receive Him, and we know that to as many as receive Him He gives the power to become sons and daughters of God. If you believe all the moves of the Spirit ceased with Bible times, you're automatically limiting what God can do in your life, and you'll stay stuck in those areas. The truth is, God wants to set you free, and He wants you to know Him intimately and deeply. He wants to give you the power to live a Spirit-filled life and live unstuck, but you must believe and have the boldness to act.

I talk to people and go to churches where they say they believe in healing. But it's odd how often I'll go to a church that believes in healing in their statement of faith . . . but they don't pray for the sick. It's fine to say you believe in something, but it takes boldness to activate what God has available to you. You can only receive the benefit of a truth of God to the degree that you will boldly go after it!

Years ago, our church was really good at doing church together—so much so we were accidentally putting out the vibe that we were so comfortable together there was no room for you to enter in. So we started to do what I call turning church inside out, and we began to go after those who did not know Jesus actively. During this time, we quit emphasizing the things of the Spirit quite so much, so we wouldn't be off-putting. We tried this experiment for a couple of years. But I tell you, it didn't do us any good to try to be more inclusive yet cease being bold with the power of God! We weren't activating the benefits of what we believed.

FEAR OF FAILURE AND FEAR OF OPINIONS WILL KEEP YOU STUCK, AS WILL PERFECTIONISM.

If you're apologetic or hesitant about acting on a truth, you either don't really believe it, or you're more afraid of what people think than interested in what God wants. This doesn't leave the Holy Spirit room to do the work He wants to in your life. Fear of failure and fear of opinions will keep you stuck, as will perfectionism. You won't always succeed the way you want and cannot please everyone all the time. Nothing will always be perfect. However, God is the God of redemption, and

He works with our failure. While we cannot please people, we can act in a way that's pleasing to God. Even though you cannot be perfect all the time, and life certainly never will be, we serve the God of refining fire who uses the very things we go through in order to make us more like His Son, Jesus.

You cannot be bold and stuck at the same time. You have to leave your stuck behind if you're going to be bold for God, and that means stepping out and being like Jesus when we get the opportunity.

Perhaps you can see how important it is to know God if you want to discern His voice from the crowd. Getting to know His Word and knowing what He is like will help you filter His voice from those of this world and the lies of our enemy. You don't want to be ignorant of the schemes to deceive you, and when you know your heavenly Father, the attempts to trick you won't work.

Not only that, knowing what He's like and how He communicates will help you in those moments when you don't have time to get alone and quiet with Him. While there may be crisis moments in which you need to hear from God right away, I have found that God also needs us to hear from Him in the moment for the benefit of others. He desires for us to act on something, what's called an "unction" in theology. We don't use that word much but think of it like this—a little spiritual nudge that prompts you to act.

You see, you aren't just in this life for yourself, and while hearing from God for you is incredibly powerful and important, it's only the tip of the iceberg of what He has for you! There's a whole world out there full of people who are not connected with our heavenly Father. They're lost and hurting in a dark and painful world, and when we can hear the voice of God and follow His lead, we can change the lives of those around us.

My challenge to you is that you not settle for learning to hear God only for you. My challenge to you is that you then be ready to act on what He tells you for the benefit of others!

RICHARD PERINCHIEF

Tuning in to the voice of God and learning to know His voice are two keys to walking in the supernatural. These are some of His most powerful tools to get you unstuck and help you live a life of freedom. But, frankly, the whole world needs His freedom! It is not His will that even one is lost, and no matter how attuned you are to the voice of God and how much you get to know Him, if you do not learn to act on what He tells you, it will do you little good.

Jesus cautioned against being one who hears but does not follow His words, but James breaks it down for us even more:

But don't just listen to God's word. You must do what it says. Otherwise, you are only fooling yourselves. For if you listen to the word and don't obey, it is like glancing at your face in a mirror. You see yourself, walk away, and forget what you look like. But if you look carefully into the perfect law that sets you free, and if you do what it says and don't forget what you heard, then God will bless you for doing it. —James 1:22-25 (NLT)

In the next chapter, James describes the futility of faith without the actions that act on that faith. "In the same way, faith by itself, if it is not accompanied by action, is dead" (James 2:17, NLT). It's not enough to just hear the voice of the Lord. You've got to follow the "unction" or prompting of God. When I try to describe to people what this is like, I use the idea of haptics. A lot of modern technology uses haptics; an Apple Watch is a great example. Several times a day, my watch doesn't make a sound, but it "taps" me.

Tap-tap. *Do you want to take a few moments to breathe?* one alert may ask. Yes, I like breathing, thank you. Tap-tap. *Your garage door just opened.* Tap-tap. *A storm is coming in.* Haptics offer a small, subtle alert to something. If you belong to Jesus Christ and you've been filled with the power of the Holy Spirit, God would like to speak with you this way. God's haptics are a little tap-tap in the spirit, a nudge. There's something to do, something to act upon. God will not compete with your noise and scream at you, but when you've spent time tuning in

and learning His voice, this little nudge can be all you need to see that He has something in the supernatural for you.

GOD'S HAPTICS ARE A LITTLE TAP-TAP IN THE SPIRIT, A NUDGE.

Some people think these must be grand things—"Thus sayeth the Lord" moments. We make it so big and complex, wanting twenty confirmations before we act. But I have found that the nudges of the Holy Spirit often seem to be small things. Tap-tap, *Say hello to that total stranger.* Tap-tap, *Pray for that person.* Tap-tap, *Talk to your coworker about her family.*

The gentle prompt of the Holy Spirit is often time-sensitive, and the opportunity may be fleeting for that specific word. When you receive it, the time has come to act on the unction of God boldly.

Will you?

Acts 4:13 says that people saw the boldness of Peter and John—the willingness to step out and act on these little nudges from God in the Spirit: "Now when they saw the boldness of Peter and John, and perceived that they were uneducated and untrained men, they marveled. And they realized that they had been with Jesus" (NKJV). They weren't educated men, and they weren't practiced speakers or influencers. People didn't notice their holy looks or fancy words; they saw their boldness as they responded to the Holy Spirit and prayed for people to be healed and set free. They could tell that these were people who had spent time with Jesus.

Have you ever noticed that we tend to sound like those we've been around? If you're a parent, chances are good you've found yourself saying, "I sound just like my parents!" You may learn to speak like an influential teacher or boss. Well, these men sounded like Jesus, and there is no higher compliment!

RICHARD PERINCHIEF

If all I taught you was how to hear the voice of God and recognize it, that would be great, but it wouldn't be enough to change the lives of others without the boldness to act on the little nudges He will give you. Jesus said of Himself, "Very truly I tell you, the Son can do nothing by himself; he can do only what he sees his Father doing because whatever the Father does the Son also does" (John 5:19, NIV).

One time, for me the bold step was . . . to do nothing. Boldly do nothing? Let me explain.

Years ago, our church was about to begin a building program for a big auditorium. We started getting ready roughly three years prior, and by April of 2007, we had obtained approval for a $6.5 million loan. It was an incredible moment when these guys drove out from Orlando to have me sign the contract, yet something in me suddenly wasn't so sure. They'd made us wait for years while we jumped through every hoop they had, but now that they were here with the paperwork, I found that I was hesitant. I needed to sleep on it.

That night I couldn't sleep. I didn't want to talk to anyone about it at first even Gail because I was experiencing a conundrum. I was stuck in the middle of one of the biggest moments of my ministry. If we built the thing, we'd have a grand new facility—and a $6.5 million mortgage—fulfilling what I'd felt was a "God thing." (I'll get into this deeper when we talk about That or Better.) But I knew I'd have no peace. I had taught people for years that the peace of God is to be our umpire, and we should never try to overrule it. However, if we didn't build, what would people think? We'd been fundraising for three years for this project, and I worried I'd lose the church if we changed plans now. No one would ever trust me again.

Thanks to godly counsel from good friends, I realized that I could not overrule God's peace. I'd have to tell the congregation the truth—that we would not be going forward with our building project. So we had a meeting, and I shared with the congregation that I was no good to them if I couldn't sleep at night because I had no peace. I didn't even know

why, so I couldn't explain any reasoning to them—just the unction of God to put the brakes on.

That was April of 2007. By May of 2007, gas prices had started to go up. By summer, real estate sales ground to a halt. By winter, the country was in a deep recession. In the following banking crisis, churches across America actually lost their buildings when banks unexpectedly called their loans due.

A friend later spoke as a guest at our church and said that he'd shared our story of not building our building all around the world. He said that while I had feared losing my credibility for changing course, I'd shown him an excellent example of not putting the fear of man before the will of God. He got a standing ovation, and I started crying—both because of his kind words and because God had preserved us from unknown troubles because we'd obeyed the unction of God.

I had felt so stuck, hopeless, and desperate. I felt like obeying God and telling the congregation we weren't going to do it was like laying my ministry on the altar as Abraham did Isaac. Yet, it was time to decide that God was more important to me even than my ministry—more than anything—and then boldly act on what He was whispering into my heart.

Boldness isn't always to act brashly; sometimes, it means you stay put. But whatever it is God calls you to do, it takes faith to act on it, whether that means standing still or stepping forward. Can you see how important it is to hear and know the voice of God and obey?

WHATEVER IT IS GOD CALLS YOU TO DO, IT TAKES FAITH TO ACT ON IT, WHETHER THAT MEANS STANDING STILL OR STEPPING FORWARD.

My hope is that you will do what you perceive your Father is doing—these little promptings and nudges from Him that indicate it's time to do what He says.

This is why I spent some time defining what ministry is and trying to establish that it's not just Clergy Man who performs ministry. Instead, we define ministry, for all of us, as "using all of your God-given talents, abilities, and resources to serve others, to fulfill the divine assignment and purpose for which you were born."

You have a divine purpose. Will you have the boldness to get unstuck and follow it?

Ocala National Forest is near where we live, and if you're familiar with Florida, you know we have wet and dry seasons. We get fires during the dry season, and one time as I was driving through a burned-out section of forest, I looked out to see seedlings coming up in orderly rows. I thought it was so cool that someone came out right on the heels of a fire and planted a new forest, but when I mentioned this to my mother, an elementary school teacher for nearly forty years, she told me that's not what had happened.

She held up an unburned pinecone. "Do you see these orderly rows?" she asked. "When a pinecone heats up in the fire, it explodes, and all these seeds shoot into the ground like somebody planted them."

"Like a grenade?" I asked her. She nodded. "How have I never heard of this?" I asked.

But a sudden idea popped into my spirit—collateral grace. You may have heard of the concept of collateral damage, where a weapon may be intended for one thing but damages something else. For example, a bomb may be intended to kill a bunch of soldiers, but a building gets destroyed or innocents killed as well. This is collateral damage.

God has something else in mind than damage—collateral grace.

Christians are bearers of collateral grace. When we go through the fire, we're like this pinecone—distributers of the grace God has stored

up inside of us. One old saying goes that Christians are like teabags: not much good unless they get in hot water.

I love the story of Paul and Silas praying and singing in the Philippian jail at midnight. They've been beaten, and the prison is likely a disgusting dungeon, yet there they are, praising God in the middle of the night. Suddenly, an earthquake hits, and everyone is set free! The verse actually says, "All the doors were opened and everyone's *chains were loosed*" (Acts 16:26 NKJV, emphasis mine).

That is you—you are a bearer of collateral grace, and when you go through the fire, you're going to explode like that pinecone full of seeds. They're seeds of God's grace and mercy that will spring up like saplings in a burned-out forest as the people around you benefit.

Sometimes, when we're stuck in the fire, all we want to do is get out of it. It hurts, and we don't like it. Yet it takes a certain amount of time for that pinecone to open in the heat. It's not enough to just get it warm; it's got to get hot.

The Bible describes God refining us in fire as a precious metal like gold or silver. In order to get rid of impurities, they heat gold in the fire until the dross rises to the top. Then, they scrape that off. They do that over and over until the metal within is as pure as possible. Isaiah 48:10 says, "See, I have refined you, though not as silver; I have tested you in the furnace of affliction" (NIV).

Peter put it like this:

So be truly glad. There is wonderful joy ahead, even though you must endure many trials for a little while. These trials will show that your faith is genuine. It is being tested as fire tests and purifies gold—though your faith is far more precious than mere gold. So when your faith remains strong through many trials, it will bring you much praise and glory and honor on the day when Jesus Christ is revealed to the whole world.
—1 Peter 1:6-7 (TPT)

Your focus may be getting out of the fire when you're stuck, but God may have something else in mind. Your suffering means something for you and for those around you who catch your collateral grace. Just as you're a Pez dispenser of hope, you're also a vehicle for God to plant His grace in the lives of those around you.

> **YOUR SUFFERING MEANS SOMETHING FOR YOU AND FOR THOSE AROUND YOU WHO CATCH YOUR COLLATERAL GRACE.**

CHAPTER 12

THAT OR BETTER

"Now faith is the substance of things hoped for, the evidence of things not seen," (Hebrews 11:1, NKJV). Faith shows the reality of what we hope for. I like to tell people that you have to be able to picture a desirable outcome (hope), and I have found many times God will give you a picture when you are stuck—something to hope for and strive for. The Bible tells us that for the joy that was set before Him, Jesus endured the cross, and I believe that we can endure being stuck when we have a picture from God to give us hope.

> **WE CAN ENDURE BEING STUCK WHEN WE HAVE A PICTURE FROM GOD TO GIVE US HOPE.**

I've also noticed something else that I alluded to in the previous chapter: as you move toward it, often what you start hoping for may not be "it." Of course, our hope is to be in God alone, but sometimes the only way He can get us to hope is to put something in our sights that we can grasp. It's a starting place. He knows we are only dust, and He knows our frailty, so I like to teach people about a concept I call That or

STUCK

Better. It's the idea that the starting place for our faith may not be what it ends up looking like in the end.

I know I've told a lot of church stories, but I feel like another one provides a great illustration of this. In 1994, our church was trying to move into a new space. We had our eyes on a shopping center, and we raised $25,000 toward this move. We had negotiated a good price on a lease, and we signed a rental agreement with the company on a Friday afternoon. The following Monday, we got a phone call that the shopping center had sold over the weekend, and the new owners would not honor our contract! They believed that the rent should be double what we'd negotiated.

We worked on this issue for weeks. We knew that we were on borrowed time at our old facility because they were going to sell it, so now we were in a bit of a frenzy. It didn't feel right. We'd been so sure that we would get the shopping center that it threw a lot of people off.

My father-in-law had just become the church's business manager, and he convinced me that before we signed a deal to pay too much in rent, we would let him look for some property. He called a wealthy friend who owned some pastureland just a few miles down the road from our church. However, though the man was open to selling, he wanted us to pay for the land in full, cash. He wouldn't accept a note. We engaged with the bank and were promised they would get us the funding in two or three months. The time passed, but while I was out of town speaking, I got a call that the bank had turned us down. It was a gut punch!

At that moment, in tears, I lifted my hands in prayer and said, "I will praise You anyway! I don't understand what's going on, but I praise You anyway." Having felt like the shopping plaza was going to be ours and then being convinced that the land would be ours, now I didn't even know if I could hear from God. Maybe I was just crazy, or perhaps I couldn't hear accurately anymore. Was I even hoping for the right things since we kept getting disappointed? However, even in that uncertainty, I was determined to trust God.

About two weeks later, the landowner called my father-in-law and said, "I thought you were going to buy it." My father-in-law told him about the bank and that we were stuck. "I'll tell you what I might do," the owner said. "How much do you have right now?" My father-in-law told him that we had $25,000. Unexpectedly, this man said that he would accept our $25,000 as a down payment, and we could pay him $30,000 annually plus interest over the next five years; he would hold the note (having just told us weeks before he didn't want a note). Miraculously, we purchased twenty-four acres of prime land on a major highway for a total of $225,000! God had made a way out of no way. Instead of a high-priced rental building, we were able to buy our own property and build equity for our future.

This turned out to be the land we are on right now!

Sometimes God shows you something, but that's not "it"—it's just a way of getting you to trust, to take a step. If we had not seen the shopping center, we would not have raised the $25,000 that ended up being enough to get the landowner to carry the remainder of the note. God had to get us moving, so He could steer us. This was not the first time God had done this, and it certainly wasn't the last.

However, He was establishing something in my heart—that or better.

If you have been stuck for a long time, it may be difficult for you to hope. Proverbs tells us, "Hope deferred makes the heart sick, but a dream fulfilled is a tree of life" (Proverbs 13:12, NLT). God understands how your heart works and how discouraged you can get when your hopes go unfulfilled. Sometimes He must jumpstart us by giving us something to hope for that doesn't end up being the ultimate destination. God has often given me a picture as a focus of my faith, but I have learned to trust in God's best—even when it's different from what I was originally picturing.

AS GOOD AS YOU CAN PICTURE IT, GOD CAN DO BETTER.

It's inspired me to routinely pray, "God, whether it's this one or not, I want your best—this or better. I claim the favor and the timing of God." And let me tell you something. As good as you can picture it, God can do better. Read this:

Never doubt God's mighty power to work in you and accomplish all this. He will achieve infinitely more than your greatest request, your most unbelievable dream, and exceed your wildest imagination! He will outdo them all, for his miraculous power constantly energizes you. Now we offer up to God all the glorious praise that rises from every church in every generation through Jesus Christ—and all that will yet be manifest through time and eternity. Amen! —Ephesians 3:20-21 (TPT)

God created you with the power to imagine a better future. We were created in His image, and we serve a God of infinite imagination and creativity. He is not bound by any limit, and He wants us to dream the best dreams imaginable. However, He understands how discouraged we can become.

Think back to Thomas and how God handled his doubts. Jesus didn't reprimand Thomas; He did one better. Thomas wanted to see His scars, but Jesus had Thomas touch the holes and know that He was no ghost or spirit but the living, breathing Son of God, raised from the dead.

I cannot tell you how many people from my congregation have come up to say to me that the principle of That or Better has impacted how they buy a house or how they handle their hopes, especially when it doesn't seem to be working out as they had pictured. Churches where I have shared this message have told me of purchases they wanted to make that were like our church's experience, where God pointed them at one thing but then gave them something better. I'm convinced that this is a powerful life principle, and to me, it's a critical concept to grasp when you're stuck. It acts to balance the fact that we may not always be perfectly tuned in to the Holy Spirit.

You might have the desired outcome in mind, but the truth is, God isn't limited to that. He may have something better for you. So, which do you want? Your preconception or God's ultimate best?

You can become stuck on your own interpretation of what God said. I didn't want to tell you about this initially until we had more of a foundation for how we hear from God, but it's important to understand that even as we tune ourselves to His voice, we are still fallible receivers. As human vessels with our biases and frailties, we will inevitably hear what God is saying yet put it through the filter of our hopes and ambitions. That is why it is vital to submit our hopes and dreams to Him.

Remember Psalm 37:4 (NKJV): "Delight yourself also in the Lord, and He shall give you the desires of your heart." This isn't about just receiving what you want; it's about letting God set your desire and vision.

So, where will you set your hope?

It's important for us to set our hopes on the right things. I like to remind people that our faith is not in what we want God to do for us; our hope is in Him and Him alone. We aren't putting our faith in the blessings, but in our Father who gives those blessings—and adds no sorrow with them!

Another saying I like came out of this prayer—a quote from a friend, Steve Kelly: "Interest gives you entrance." Steve is my pastor and dear friend, and he said this because he often finds that God gives us access to the desires He has placed in our hearts.

I am a passionate college football fan, and I especially love the Florida Gators and have since I was a kid. I was introduced to Dwayne Thomas, who intercepted a pass when the Gators faced the Florida State Seminoles in the late '90s, sealing the win. I remembered that game a decade later when I met him because I could remember barely being able to preach the next day. I had been screaming my head off with excitement during the game! Dwayne was one of the chaplains for the Gators at that time, and as I got to know him, he came to meet with me for lunch a few times. Our connection eventually ended up with me having the

opportunity to do a chapel service in the off-season and hang out with the Gators' head coach, Urban Meyer. It was so exciting, a dream come true, to be having breakfast with Coach Meyer and other leaders in the program, and a few weeks later, I had the surprise opportunity to be in the running for the next chaplain for the Gators!

While I was on vacation, I got a call that it wasn't going to work out after all. Terry Jackson, another famous Florida Gator, told me that he really wanted someone who was African American to be the chaplain. I was disappointed for a moment and thought about arguing that I had a mostly Black church. But then I had another thought—Pastor Lindsey, my son in the faith, is an incredible man of God. So I suggested him to Jackson, and he loved the idea.

I gave Pastor Lindsey a call, but he was initially reluctant because he was so busy. Finally, however, I told him that it was an incredible opportunity and that Coach Meyer wanted to meet with him.

"I've got a foul mouth, and I'm not changing," Meyer told him. "Can you live with that?"

"Coach, I don't know who you think you're talking to," Lindsey told him, "but I'm not here for anything. I'm not here with an agenda, and I don't need your money. If you want me, I'm open, but I'm not here to change you. I'm here to help these kids—that's it." Coach Meyer loved it!

My son in the faith, the incredible psalmist and worship leader that God had blessed me with, stepped into an entrance that my interest in football opened—not for me, but for him. He was able to be the chaplain for the Florida Gators during the Tim Tebow years, and he influenced the lives of dozens of young, promising athletes.

You could say that not getting to be the chaplain myself was a disappointment, but the fact is that God had something better in mind. My heart's desire for sports, which I had submitted to Him, gave God the opportunity to reach into the players' lives and influence them for Christ through Pastor Lindsey for three incredible years.

I want you to see this because you must understand your hopes and dreams are not just for you. I know you want freedom, but not even getting unstuck is just for you. Your hopes and dreams are tied to the lives of others, and it is God's heart to see you succeed greatly. Remember, Jesus told us that we would do even greater things than He did! That is part of God's heart for you, and I want you to begin to see your circumstances (stuck or not) through this lens—it's not just about you. God wants you free, but He also wants to use you to help others be free as well.

I have been telling you to submit your ways to the Lord, acknowledge Him, and give Him your hope and desires. He will guide your steps and direct your path, making it straight to Him because you were humble enough to put your faith and hope in Him. He wants you to trust that the desires that He puts in your heart will be more ultimately fulfilling than anything you can cook up on your own. He wants you to shake off the selfish idea that it is all about you.

If you're stuck and discouraged, having put your hope in things that didn't pan out, I urge you to honestly submit those hopes to Him and ask if they're genuinely where He wants you to put your faith. If your heart has grown sick because of deferred hope, it's time to do a hope check and look ahead to what may be coming next from your loving heavenly Father. His plans for you are good, and they are plans that will put hope in your heart. They may not be what you expect, and the ultimate blessing He has for you may not be what you think it will be at first. So be willing to look for the That or Better and trust that He will use the desires He is putting in you, even if you don't see the fulfillment now—even if the greater impact is actually on another life than your own.

We began this chapter with Hebrews 11, the unforgettable chapter of the Bible that shows us God's Faith Hall of Fame. It's full of people like Noah, Abraham, and Moses who lived to see incredible promises of God come to pass. But none of them saw the ultimate destination of what they hoped for. Instead, they saw it all from a distance, trusting God.

They were looking for a better place than this fallen earth, a heavenly homeland, to the point that Abraham was even willing to offer Isaac, the son of promise, as an offering to God, utterly convinced that God could bring his son and his dreams back from the dead!

What hopes do you have that seemed like promises for your future but now seem dead? What desires are in your heart that God has yet to fulfill? I have urged you to write things down before because that works for me, so right now, why don't you take a moment to write out some of these unfulfilled hopes.

Now, read Hebrews 11. Read about the faith of the patriarchs and the miracles that God did for His people. By faith, they conquered, ruled, and received a portion of what God had promised them. You'll read that for some, lions did not eat them; for others, flames didn't burn them. Some escaped death at the point of a sword. They became strong, and some even received loved ones back from the dead! Sounds good, right?

Yet read on. Others didn't get what they asked for. Instead, they were tried and tortured, mocked and beaten, chained and imprisoned, and many other heroes of the faith did not see what they hoped for come to pass. Does this mean God was unfaithful to them? Hebrews 11:39-40 (TPT) describes them:

> *These were the true heroes, commended for their faith, yet they lived in hope without receiving the fullness of what was promised them. But now God has invited us to live in something better than what they had—faith's fullness! This is so that they could be brought to finished perfection alongside of us.*

Having read that, what do you feel about your deferred hope? Is God unfaithful when He lets us feel stuck? And, do you still believe it's always a bad thing when you feel stuck? Could it be that God can use any circumstance to lead you to something better that He has envisioned for your life?

You might remember that at the beginning of this book, I told you that I never wanted to be a pastor. In fact, I fought it! However, God

RICHARD PERINCHIEF

knew what would bring me fulfillment, and He guided my steps into ministry. Remember, I wanted to be a rock 'n' roll star or perhaps a media personality. I became neither; I became something better.

Right now, you want to be unstuck. I don't blame you! Being stuck is horrible, or at least it can be when we focus on the problem right in front of our nose. Yet, being stuck may mean that you are on pause or waiting on God for something better than what you've been dreaming about. And it may not even be for you—it might be for those who come after you.

God is not trying to make you eat your broccoli, forcing you into something you don't want. After all, I didn't want to be a pastor, but I didn't truly understand what that meant when I shot down the idea as a teenager. If I had known then what I know now, I would've welcomed whatever God wanted me to dream.

Don't rule out any dreams that God puts in your heart. You may think it needs to look special and sacred, but God's plan for you may not have anything to do with full-time ministry or anything else that seems to check all the nice little Christian boxes. God isn't limited to the four walls of the church or to the acts of a nonprofit; God is in it all. The church isn't to be a monastery, sheltering us within its walls; it's an embassy, reaching out through people who know God into any and every dream He has for His kids. You are called to invade the enemy's territory, to bring a lifestyle of God's ideas and breakthroughs and freedom in creative and unexpected ways to those who do not know Him. They may not be what you pictured them as originally.

They'll be better.

I told you about Pastor Lindsey getting to be the chaplain for the Florida Gators, but there are so many other things that God has done through another person because He put a desire in my heart. Interest gave entrance to Pastor Lindsey, but I believe it also did so for my son, Ricky, and others in our church.

STUCK

I grew up in a musical family. In fact, my parents met in college because of a shared interest in classical choral music. Though both became teachers as their vocation, Dad completed his master's and doctorate degrees in music education, and Mom completed her master's degree as well. They were always very involved in singing in church choirs as well as leading choral music at the college level as well as in the community.

My earliest memories were sitting in the audience proudly watching and listening to my folks as they opened their mouths wide and brought forth beautiful melodies. Consequently, music got into my blood and nearly every Christmas and birthday, I received presents relating to it. For some reason, I've always loved the drums and admired the gifted drummers I saw growing up. But strangely I never learned to play the drums myself. I took several years of piano lessons, played the trombone for all of middle school and into high school and became a part of a rock and roll garage band singing lead and playing bass guitar. By the time adulthood responsibilities set in, I pretty much sold all my instruments to keep food on the table.

When our son, Ricky, was born, we noticed early on that he had great rhythm. Every day he would open our kitchen drawer full of pots and pans and set them up into a little drum set. By the age of two, my in-laws bought him his first junior drum kit. At six, we got him a little electric drum pad set, which he played so well he was invited to play along with the kids' worship team from church. At eleven, he became the regular drummer at our church and continues there every few weeks to this day.

Ironically, our associate pastor, Chris Hays, was a fantastic drummer. When Pastor Lindsey first arrived, his primary instrument was drums, and when our youth pastor (who is our son-in-law, Tristan Kennedy) joined the team, we discovered he also was a drummer. At one point, it kind of hit me that I'm surrounded by drummers. For some reason, my life is like a drummer magnet. Is it possible that my great interest has given me entrance into the rhythm of God's wonderful creation of music?

By the way, one night we had all our percussionists lead a segment of drums-only worship and praise. The psalmists of old would have marveled.

I was in heaven, and I didn't play a note. Yet even though I wasn't the one playing, my heart could not grow any bigger seeing those I love step into something from my heart because of God's blessing. I think this should give us a glimpse of understanding into the heart of our Father God. You who are parents understand this—it is your joy to give things to your children.

Mr. Holland's Opus, starring Richard Dreyfuss, is one of my favorite movies of all time. Since my father was a music professor, this movie touched me personally, and I just sobbed when I saw it. It's similar to my father's story.

In the movie, Richard Dreyfuss played a man in the '60s who wanted to write a symphony but could not pay his bills. He got married and had a baby, but it was a trial because their child was deaf and couldn't hear his father's music. Mr. Holland ended up becoming a music teacher. He went through years and years of frustration, feeling like he was wasting his life. Suddenly, he was sixty years old. His school downsized and cut funding, and he was forced into early retirement.

On his last day, he heard a noise in the auditorium. His wife and son, acting like they didn't know what was going on, urged him to check it out. He walked in to find his former students and their families, as well as the entire school, it seemed, all gathered together—including one little girl who used to play the clarinet and had no confidence but had become governor of the state!

"We finished your symphony," she told him. But it gets better.

Indicating all the former students whose lives he'd changed, the governor said, "You don't know it, but we are your symphony." He was invited to the podium to conduct the ragtag orchestra made up of his

former students from three decades of his life playing the opus he'd only heard in his head. He was ecstatic as he led the symphony playing his music, which he thought was a dream that went unfulfilled. Yet it was a dream that his true symphony—the kids whose lives he changed—fulfilled in a way he could never have dreamed of.

I love the story because Holland thought he was stuck the whole time. He felt like he was not fulfilling his purpose as he taught music to generation after generation of kids. But, at the end of his career, he had impacted all those lives who stood up to celebrate him!

You may feel you are stuck because your dreams have not come true, but I would challenge you that God is working in the winter, and you may not be able to see the real fruit He wants to bring from your life. If your focus is just on getting unstuck, you may miss the point. God's dreams for you are bigger than that.

> **IF YOUR FOCUS IS JUST ON GETTING UNSTUCK, YOU MAY MISS THE POINT. GOD'S DREAMS FOR YOU ARE BIGGER THAN THAT.**

God is not a puppet master, pulling your strings to get you to dance. Some Christian circles debate man's free will or God's sovereignty, but I want to tell you that it is not one or the other—it's both! God asks you to dance with Him and move as He leads and directs your steps. You may not know where He is going or how you will get there, but He is leading you into something good—something that will be better for you and others than what your limited human mind can imagine.

Yes, this book is about getting unstuck, but me trying to teach you these keys means little if you misunderstand the heart of our Father and His mindset. His view is not limited to the end of your nose; He considers all of eternity and the lives of those around you. Yet He is mindful of your frame and limitations and knows that hope deferred will make your heart sick. He balances both.

You may feel like you're just existing, as though you are stuck like Mr. Holland in a job that is less than the fulfillment of your dreams. But I am telling you that if you open your heart to God's perspective, He can enlarge the scope of your vision and dominion to encompass things that you haven't even thought of yet and impact lives that may not even exist at this moment. You might be focused on just surviving, just getting out of the bad place that you feel like you're in right now, but God may have dreams for you to transform nations!

You have a critical choice. You can choose to see your situation through the limits of your own perspective and vision. Or you can put your faith in God and have hope that His plan for you is better, more fulfilling, more complete, and broader than anything you can cook up on your own. The first thing He directs your heart toward may not be the thing, but if you keep your heart sensitive and tied closely to Him through relationship, He can guide and direct your steps into His ultimate purposes for your life.

Right now, you may be reading all this with a sick feeling in the pit of your stomach that you are like sixty-year-old Mr. Holland. You may fear that you have wasted your life, stuck. But let me just tell you, it is never ever too late!

You already know that I love Joshua from the Bible because of our core scripture from Joshua 1 that God is always with us and will never forsake or abandon us. However, another story from the life of Joshua also stands out. In this one, Israel had screwed up and done something that God had told them not to. Tricked, they made a covenant with a people from the land of Canaan when God had told them to destroy these people. Should they go back on a binding covenant to obey God? They probably felt pretty stuck.

You might think that God would leave them hanging because of their sin—because they'd done the wrong thing and made their bed. Now, it was time to sleep in it, right? So, when several kings came to attack Israel and their tricky new allies, I think we could all understand if Joshua wondered if God would be with them.

Yet, God had promised to give them the land. He had promised to be with them and not abandon them. You may also remember that God repeatedly told Joshua to be courageous and strong. In this situation, we can see one of the reasons why God said it and then repeated it—because Joshua would face uncertainty and trial.

In the face of a seemingly overwhelming force, a coalition of kings and cities set to destroy them, Joshua sought the Lord. Perhaps as David did many years later, Joshua knew that he needed to hear from God. "'Do not be afraid of them,' the Lord said to Joshua, 'for I have given you victory over them. Not a single one of them will be able to stand up to you'" (Joshua 10:8, NLT). With that word in his heart and vision in his eyes, Joshua and Israel attacked their enemies, coming upon them suddenly after marching all night.

Sometimes we read these stories without really thinking about them, but just stop and consider how tired we would be after marching all night. Think about the humans involved in this Bible story, their frailties, doubts, and fears.

Now, add God to the mix.

The Bible tells us that the Lord routed Israel's enemies before them, and the people of God slaughtered their foes as God even destroyed them with hailstones—more dying from God than the Israelites' swords! Yet, they chased their enemies so long, and it took so long to destroy them, that for a while, it seemed as though the Lord's promise that no one would be left to stand against them would fail. They were tired, having marched all night to a battle they may not even have been "supposed" to fight.

Have you ever felt like that? Have you ever felt like you were stuck or in a bad place because of your own decisions? Maybe you felt like you had to pick between more than one bad choice, as though there were not a good choice to be made. Now, you find yourself feeling stuck because of layer after layer of questionable decisions that led you to the place you are today. Does that mean that God is no longer with you? Though He gave you a vision, you have yet to see it happen, or it is not lining up like you pictured it.

You are not alone. You have never been. I have felt the same way, and Joshua no doubt felt that way on this historic day. Yet, all those questions and doubts did not keep Joshua from praying one of the boldest prayers in the entire Bible—not in private, but in front of the whole body of Israel: "Sun, stand still over Gibeon; and Moon, in the Valley of Aijalon" (Joshua 10:12b, NKJV).

And it happened!

God honored that bold prayer, and the day did not end; the sun and moon stayed in place until God's promise was fulfilled, and Israel had defeated her enemies. There's never been a day like it, but surely the Lord fought for His children that day!

He has not stopped fighting for His kids. He fights for you still.

Not a day goes by that you are lost or forgotten, and no matter what you have done or what failures seem to haunt your past, God and His dreams for your life will not be dissuaded. He who began a good work in you is faithful to bring it to completion, and since He authored your faith, He will be faithful to finish it.

> **NOT A DAY GOES BY THAT YOU ARE LOST OR FORGOTTEN, AND NO MATTER WHAT YOU HAVE DONE OR WHAT FAILURES SEEM TO HAUNT YOUR PAST, GOD AND HIS DREAMS FOR YOUR LIFE WILL NOT BE DISSUADED.**

STUCK

You may feel like you're stuck, but I urge you to cultivate a sense of hope that not only can God work to prepare you in the cold winter months, but His dream for your summer is better than anything you could hope for or dream! He is not discouraged, and His promises have not been thwarted. Just as He gave Israel the Promised Land, He is rolling out a promising future for you—in fact, it's His best! It includes you, but it even goes beyond you.

Dear reader, let your hope be renewed! Don't place it in what you want God to do for you. Instead, recognize that it's only the starting place. God may have given you a target to believe for, but that is not the end, especially if it has not gone according to your plan. Believe it or not, that's okay.

God's plan is better than yours.

Joshua prayed a bold prayer, and right now, I want to encourage you to do the same thing. In the context of a relationship with God, ask His Holy Spirit to show you how to pray. Then, I encourage you to get out a pen and paper and write out a bold prayer to God inspired by Joshua's.

Then, have hope in God that He will fight for His kid (you) and show His faithfulness. Believe for what you're asking of Him—but hold on because it may be that. Or it may be better!

CHAPTER 13

SHOW THEM HOW TO BE FREE

In these last few chapters, I've tried to lean into something that can be hard to hear when you're stuck—that it's not all about you. Sometimes, when we feel trapped, all we can think about is getting free of our situation. Yet, I want to bring you one of the most important keys that keeps so many people stuck: Selfishness.

I hear a public service announcement occasionally where people discuss the reasons why they want to quit smoking. One is funny—an older lady talking about how she is quitting for the sake of her dog. However, another is very moving as a man explains that his son is actually his reason to quit smoking. If it were all just about him, maybe he'd continue to light 'em up. But, now that his son has entered the world, he's motivated to get healthier so that his son won't grow up without a father. This man wants to be there to see his son graduate and get married, so he's willing to do something he does not want to do.

Let me ask you this: What's your motive for getting unstuck? Is it just so it'll quit being uncomfortable and inconvenient? That is legitimate, as being stuck is miserable. But let's dig a little deeper. How does your situation of being stuck impact your spouse? Your kids? Your extended

family? What about friends and coworkers? If you just want freedom for yourself, you can be missing powerful motivations and inspirations that will actually help to set you free.

Yet that's only part of it. You can still be selfishly motivated because in a way these are still "your" people. Let's go another step deeper. There's a whole world of stuck people out there—hurting people who have lost their hope and countless others who have not yet found their ultimate source of hope in Jesus. God wants you free, dear reader, but not just for your sake—He wants you free so that you can then act as the hands and feet of Jesus on this planet and help free others.

We are sons and daughters of the King; we're royalty because of our Father. I like to remind people of this in my preaching because it calls us upward in our thinking. However, just as important is that we are to be like our example, Jesus, who did not come to be served but to serve and to pour out His life for many. We are to pour out our lives like a drink offering, to follow in His footsteps as servants.

What better way to serve others than to show them how to be free?

Perhaps you've experienced something like this—you feel down, depressed, and are focused on something negative going on in your life. Then, someone calls or messages you with a problem, and instantly, you shift gears to try to encourage this friend or loved one. I've heard moms, especially, turn on a dime and go from crying to cheerful, all because their kids were hurting or in trouble and needed their moms' support. In an instant, the depression is gone, replaced by the desire to encourage another.

Ephesians 6:8 (TPT) tells us to "be assured that anything you do that is beautiful and excellent will be repaid by our Lord." In other words, if you do it for someone else, you don't have to look to them to pay you back; God will repay you.

When you're stuck, looking beyond yourself can be one of the hardest things to do. But, when you're stuck, one of the most powerfully freeing things you can possibly do is help another find their freedom! One of the best ways to get unstuck... is to help someone else get unstuck.

If you've been in Christian circles long enough, you've probably heard a preacher say to give out of your need. However, where many of them are talking about money, I'm talking about something different. It seems counterintuitive, but sometimes to break us free, we need to give the exact thing we feel like we're lacking.

My mom grew up in an old house in New Jersey—we're talking over 120 years old. In the back, there was an old pump, and the crazy thing about this pump was that in order to get water from the well, you had to prime the pump. Many of us have heard the expression, but the practice looked like this: you had to put a little water into the pump before you could use the pump to get more water. You see, it moistened the seals and gaskets that would otherwise be dry and unable to function.

This is a principle that goes back to the Old Testament, and I like the example where Elijah prophesied a drought. At first, God took care of him divinely, sending him food. Eventually, even that provision dried up, and God sent the prophet to a poor widow. Elijah asked her for a drink. Remember, they were in a drought—and as she was going to get it, he asked if she'd bring him a bite of bread, too.

This widow told him that she didn't have a single thing to eat in her house, only a little flour and oil left before she and her son would starve and die. And he wanted her to give him her last bite? This seems incredibly selfish of him, but here's why it's so important to be connected to the voice of God: this was the act that would set her free.

Elijah told her, "Don't be afraid," and go do what she had planned—but first give him a bite of bread (1 Kings 17:13, NKJV). Then, he gave her a word from the Lord: "For thus says the Lord God of Israel: 'The bin of flour shall not be used up, nor shall the jar of oil run dry, until the day the Lord sends rain on the earth'" (1 Kings 17:14, NKJV).

STUCK

Just imagine this situation, a staring contest between a destitute widow and a prophet of God. She had just told him they're dying, and he asked her for bread. Perhaps, after looking at him a while, she finally decided, "What's another day going to matter?"

Whatever her reasoning, she did it. She baked him some bread first, and when she was done, something amazing happened—there was still some oil and flour left. In fact, after they ate that day, there was still some left. And the next day, and the next day! The man of God stayed there in her home, blessing her family, for many days after, and the flour and oil never ran out!

You may feel stuck; you may feel empty. You may feel as though you have nothing at all to give. But if you'll listen to the voice of God when He tells you to give, you may find that the very thing He is asking of you is the very thing that He wants to give to you. If the widow hadn't made the bread, what would've happened? Perhaps Elijah would've gone on to bless another widow and her family. We'll never know because she obeyed the voice of God.

What are you missing out on that God wants to give you? What freedom and blessing does He want to give another through you? Your time, attention, encouragement, passion, or comfort may be exactly what helps get someone else unstuck.

In another powerful story in the Old Testament, a woman came to Elisha, Elijah's successor, and asked for his help. Her sons were about to be sold into slavery to pay her late husband's debt. Elisha asked her, "What do you have in the house?" And she said, "Your maidservant has nothing in the house but a jar of oil" (2 Kings 4:2, NKJV).

He told her to gather as many jars as she could and to go into her home, shut the door, and begin to pour out the little bit that she had. Just like the widow and Elijah, something incredible happened—as she poured, the oil kept coming, and coming, until eventually they ran out of jars to fill! She sold the oil to not only pay her debt but also live on the rest.

When we were commuting back and forth to Orlando, there was a gap between the morning and evening services, and we'd go to a buffet called Ryan's Steakhouse almost every week with a group of others from our church. We didn't have a lot of money, but we'd worked out how we could feed all four of us for a little over $12!

One weekend, we were particularly tight financially. I had $13 in my wallet. We'd already tithed, but the pastor was speaking about giving God's best, and I felt like the Lord told me to give $3. Now, this isn't much, but I knew Ryan's was $12. If I gave three, we wouldn't have enough for lunch. Gail and I felt like we were to give it (though she didn't know how much I had in my wallet).

We told our friends we'd see them at Ryan's, and as we pulled into the parking lot, Gail asked, "How much did you give?" I told her $3. "How much did we have?" I told her I'd had $13. So, we decided we'd go ahead and show up, but we'd then tell our friends we wouldn't be going in because we'd forgotten something we needed to do.

However, as we opened the car door, a friend shouted out, "Hey, I'm glad you're here!" I asked him why, and with a big smile, he replied, "Because the Lord spoke to me on the way over and told me to bless you with a great steak dinner!" He wouldn't hear of us doing our usual penny-pinching; he insisted we get the prime rib!

And, while we were there, another friend came up and said, "I just want to do something for you," and gave us $30. So, not only did we get blessed with a wonderful steak dinner, we went home with thirty extra dollars in cash in our pockets!

When God tells you He knows what you need and will take care of you, it means He knows what you need—to eat, to drive, to live in. He is not limited. But He also understands that it's not enough to simply take you out of slavery and set you free; He has to get the slavery out of you! Giving, especially when we feel like we have nothing, is one of the most powerful ways He does this.

STUCK

> **GOD UNDERSTANDS THAT IT'S NOT ENOUGH TO SIMPLY TAKE YOU OUT OF SLAVERY AND SET YOU FREE; HE HAS TO GET THE SLAVERY OUT OF YOU!**

Sometimes, the very thing you feel like you do not have much of is the very thing God wants you to give. It's the principle of sowing and reaping, and every farmer knows it—you must plant what you have in the ground in order to grow more.

How often do we limit God because we're not willing to use the little bit we have to free Him to give us more? This is how selfishness will hold you captive. You can hold back the very thing that God wants to use to set you free.

Right now, I want you to ask yourself: *What do I have in my "house"? What small something do I have that God wants me to use by giving it away?* Maybe it's your time. Maybe it's your energy. Perhaps you have knowledge or passion. Whatever it is, I urge you to sit down quietly with your notebook and prayerfully ask God what He would have you plant now that will yield a harvest later.

Once, God famously asked Moses, "What's in your hand?" He was referring to Moses's staff, and God had him throw it down, at which point it turned into a snake! Then, God told him to reach down and pick it up by the tail (which everyone in Florida knows is a good way to get bitten). Yet, Moses obeyed, and it turned back into a shepherd's staff. God used this sign to warn the Egyptians, but later He used it in Moses's hand as he stretched it out over the Red Sea.

You want to talk about stuck? The Israelites were stuck—between the Red Sea on one side and the vengeful Egyptian army on the other. And God used this symbol of Moses's authority, his staff—the very thing

Moses had leaned on instead of God for forty years—to change Moses's dependence on himself and the way he'd done things to complete and utter dependence on God.

God wanted to bring His children into the Promised Land, but first He needed to free them, once and for all, from the Egyptians. God told Moses to raise his staff, and He did one of the greatest Old Testament miracles. He parted the Red Sea. Not only did He deliver His people from Egypt, God used this situation—which seemed like the ultimate stuck between a rock and a hard place—to destroy the Egyptian army utterly and completely.

God wants to do that in you. He wants you to know what you have—thus, the inventory questions (because He already knows the answers). He wants to set you free, not just to get you out of captivity, but to utterly and completely destroy your enemies.

Let me lay it out for you again: you may wonder why God has allowed you to be stuck. Sometimes, His purpose is to show you His power by crushing your enemies so thoroughly that they can never harm you, or anyone else, again.

Is it possible, right now, that God wants to do a Red Sea moment in your life? When you think you're stuck for no good reason, look for God working behind the scenes, in your winter, to prepare you for overwhelming victory!

Butchering an old expression, God could take the children of Israel out of Egypt, but He must also take the Egypt out of the children of Israel. That would not happen until forty years after the deliverance at the Red Sea. It took that long for the people to get free of Egypt's influence, and those who could not be set free actually died in the wilderness. It also set up our boy Joshua to lead them into the Promised Land because all those years later they were stuck again, outside the promise looking in.

The old has to pass away; leave it behind. It needs to die, and you can leave it in the wilderness because you're stepping into something new.

STUCK

The new is relationship with God. He wants to take you out of captivity, but He must also take the captivity out of you, and for that, helping others and leaving selfishness behind is the key to your freedom.

It's not a question of whether or not you'll ever get stuck again; you will. The question is, will you keep up the lifestyle of connection with God you've established, so He can free you again?

> **IT'S NOT A QUESTION OF WHETHER OR NOT YOU'LL EVER GET STUCK AGAIN; YOU WILL. THE QUESTION IS, WILL YOU KEEP UP THE LIFESTYLE OF CONNECTION WITH GOD YOU'VE ESTABLISHED, SO HE CAN FREE YOU AGAIN?**

Your fear and confusion, the lies that hold you back, what others try to force you into—God has a plan for destroying all of them. They are your enemies, and they are God's enemies! Your dead Moseses can't hold you back, and neither can the things others say or do that are outside of your control. Even fatigue and disappointment cannot keep you from the freedom God has for you. In fact, no power on or below the earth, or of the enemy can stop God's work in your life or separate you from His love.

However, there is one thing that can prevent you from experiencing freedom: you.

I want to be careful here because the power of God does not lessen or wane just because you don't want to participate. And I don't want to *should* all over you by making a list of what your responsibilities are in this process and what you must do.

Instead, here's what I want for you—I want you to stretch out your faith. Believe that God is able and willing to set you free. Be willing to lay your selfishness aside so that God can use whatever He has put in you, even if it seems small and weak, to be a step toward others becoming free as well. These are my prayers for you!

When you picked up this book, you may have been looking for a magic solution to your problem; something you could just do to get free. Instead, I want you to see that it's not about the solution; it's about the relationship.

I told you about the time God gave me a word that He would give us a place with fresh paint and new carpet. But I've since learned, of much greater importance than that condo was the way God gave me the answer. Down on my face on the floor with my notebook, I learned to connect with the King of kings and the Lord of lords. He is not your Easy button or the genie in your lamp; He is your loving heavenly Father. He wants good things for you, and He has a plan. His desire is to walk you through it, one step at a time shining His light right in front of your feet.

It may surprise you, but God's ultimate goal is not getting you unstuck.

His goal is for you to know Him. God wants you to connect with the One who has not only your freedom but also freedom for any who call on His name to be saved.

So many people search for the meaning of life. They look for how to get free and find their purpose and calling. It's one of the greatest proofs that there is a God; if we were just lumps evolving from amoebas into some higher form of life, why would we feel we need a purpose? We feel this way because we have a spirit, and we know this life is not all there is.

We were not designed to be broken apart from Him and separated. On the contrary, we were created to be in fellowship with our Father.

One of the greatest lies the enemy has ever told is that, currently, most people are closed off to Jesus Christ. It's just not true! It's a lie, and, right now, people are far more open than you realize, especially post-COVID-19 because they have seen the darkness, and they have questions. They're dissatisfied, broken, and lost, and they desire to become unstuck at more than just an emotional level—they want

freedom at a supernatural level, in their spirits. Their existential questions have answers that only God can provide, and you, as His child, are positioned in their lives to be part of God's answer to them.

Getting unstuck isn't just for you. It's also for them.

The fields of lost and hurting people are ripe for harvest. There is no lack of need or openness; the shortage we have is in laborers who will go out into the harvest fields and be the answers to the questions burning in people's hearts.

They hunger for purpose and meaning, and they're desperate to get unstuck in a way that only Jesus Christ can fulfill. If you are willing to build bridges of love and trust in Jesus, you will find that people see your freedom and love and hunger for what you have.

Many Christians are afraid of being mocked or rejected. They've bought into the lie that people don't want the freedom we've found in Jesus. As I mentioned before, I used to make fun of Christians; I know what we face firsthand. It wasn't because I hated God; it's because I didn't know Him yet. People who are bullies or mockers don't know what else to do, and they're afraid and frustrated with being stuck separated from God.

Eternity hangs in the balance, and while you may think that they do not care about your testimony and your personal story of how God freed you from the power of sin and death, you'd be wrong. They've seen death intimately, and their lives of sin aren't getting them the results they desire. They've seen their world shaken, and many feel more lost and stuck than ever.

So are you willing to be a harvester? Are you ready to share the freedom you've found and to show others how to find the connection with God that will allow them to be free spiritually and in every other way? hat's the question. I'm not asking you to be a pastor in a pulpit or to become an evangelist and travel from city to city or country to country. But I am asking you if you are willing to use your God-given talents, abilities, and resources to serve others, to fulfill the divine assignment and purpose for which you were born.

This is the path that God set out. There is a path to the supernatural, as we've seen, where you learn to listen, discern, and act on the voice of God. But there is also a path to freedom, not just by hearing God's voice and acting on it for yourself but also by being willing to act on the unction of God for the sake of others.

YOUR LIFE IS MEANT TO ATTRACT LOST, STUCK PEOPLE.

Are you willing to be a carrier of the gospel, the hope of the world, and give a reason for hope every time you're asked? That's what the Bible asks—not that you beat people over the head with your Bible, but that every time you're asked, you share the reason for your hope. Your life is meant to attract lost, stuck people.

Jesus put it like this:

You're here to be light, bringing out the God-colors in the world. God is not a secret to be kept. We're going public with this, as public as a city on a hill. If I make you light-bearers, you don't think I'm going to hide you under a bucket, do you? I'm putting you on a light stand. Now that I've put you there on a hilltop, on a light stand—shine! Keep open house; be generous with your lives. By opening up to others, you'll prompt people to open up with God, this generous Father in heaven. —Matthew 5:14-16 (MSG)

God didn't create you to be stuck; He made you free! And when you've tasted that freedom, it is His hope—and mine—that you will want it for others. So, if you've been holding back, I urge you to break free, and act on every opportunity God gives you to be the light of the world!

STUCK

Are you ready to be unstuck? Great! Now, go out and help others find their freedom as well!

Throughout the Word, God delivered His people in various mighty ways, but He rarely did it the same way twice. I mentioned Moses' staff before, and it's important to note that one time God had him strike a rock which then gushed water. Another time, God told Moses to speak to the rock. Yet, in his anger over all the stuck people God had entrusted to him, Moses struck the rock again instead.

In fact, because Moses was stuck in the idea that God would deliver them again the same way He had last time and did not listen to God's instruction, leadership of Israel needed to pass to the man who would not assume he had God's formula down and who would stay in the tent of meeting in order to get the answers.

Joshua.

"Moses my servant is dead. Therefore, the time has come for you to lead these people, the Israelites, across the Jordan River into the land I am giving them. . . . No one will be able to stand against you as long as you live. For I will be with you as I was with Moses. I will not fail you or abandon you." —Joshua 1:25 (NLT)

Your "Moses" is dead. The time has come for you to lead yourself and others into the promise God has for them. It's not just about freedom, though that's a large part of it.

It's *relationship*.

Getting unstuck is not about a formula, God snapping His fingers, or you always getting what you want for yourself. It's about you connecting with God in such a way that He not only creates ways of setting you free each time you get stuck, but He can use you as a vessel, as a messenger, as an illustration of His life-giving power to set all of us free.

You, my friend, are a Joshua. You are a leader, and you are a living testimony of God's power to free His people over and over again. It's time to arise and go, knowing that wherever you go and whatever you do, He is with you. No matter what holds you now or what may try to do so in the future, God is in the business of setting the captives free and giving good gifts to His children.

He wants to give these gifts to you, but He also wishes to give them to others through you. All the days of your life, He will be with you, as He was with Moses and the other heroes of the Bible.

Be strong and courageous, and step into the freedom that comes from being unstuck.

A Prophetic Call for Personal Change!

Why live like an artificial when you were designed to be an original?

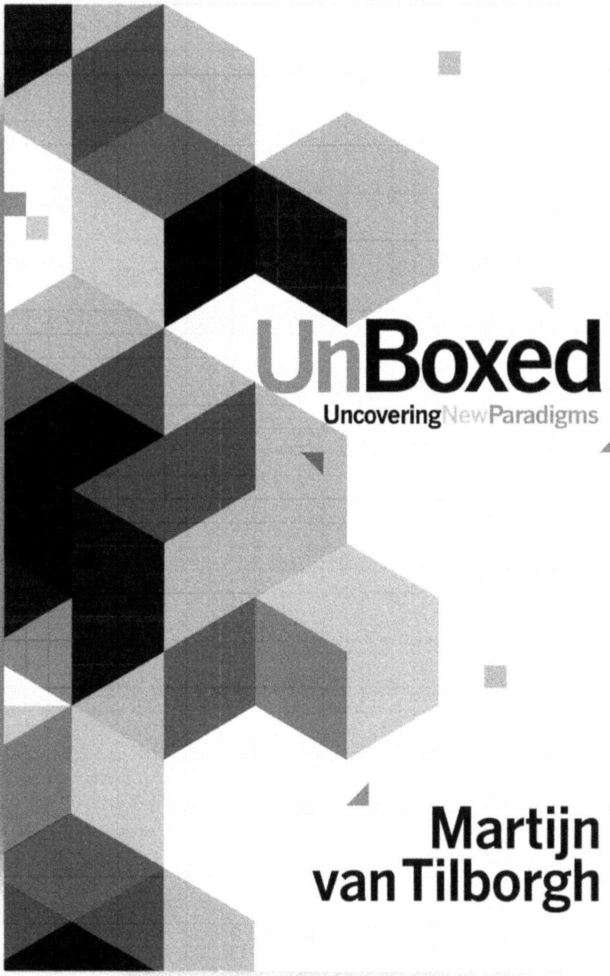

UnBoxed
Uncovering New Paradigms

"Martijn challenges you to be curious about the future, and become an explorer to discover new lands and fresh opportunities."

Martijn van Tilborgh

TO PURCHASE VISIT

THEARTOFLEADERSHIP.COM/UNBOXED

AVAIL +

TRY FOR 30 DAYS AND RECEIVE
THE SEQUENCE TO SUCCESS
BUNDLE FREE

$79 VALUE

+ BOOK
+ STUDY GUIDE
+ ONLINE COURSE
+ LIVE CLASS
+ MORE

The Art *of* Leadership

This isn't just another leadership collective...this is the next level of networking, resources, and empowerment designed specifically for leaders like you.

Whether you're an innovator in ministry, business, or your community, **AVAIL +** is designed to take you to your next level. Each one of us needs connection. Each one of us needs practical advice. Each one of us needs

THEARTOFLEADERSHIP.COM/CHAND

FOLLOW THE LEADER

STAY  CONNECTED

 facebook.com/TheArtofAvail   @theartofavail

www.ingramcontent.com/pod-product-compliance
Lightning Source LLC
Chambersburg PA
CBHW070537090426
42735CB00013B/3006